Day Trading for Beginners 2020

How to Day Trade Stocks and Forex for a Living, Learn Trading Investing Successfully Using Basic Strategies and Right Mindset

Table of Contents

Introduction

Chapter 1: The Basic Concepts of Day Trading

   What Is Day Trading?

   How Day Trading Works?

   Day Trading vs. Swing Trading

      Buy Long Sell Short

   Day Trading vs. Long Term Investing

   Benefits of Day Trading

   Downsides of Day Trading

Chapter 2: The Dos and Don'ts of Day Trading

   Basic Day Trading Tips

   The Do's of Day Trading Business

   The Don'ts of Day Trading

Chapter 3: The Main Tools of Day Trading

   The Tools

   The Trading Community

Online Trading Tools

- Tradingview
- Stockcharts
- MT4

Chapter 4: Choosing the Right Stock to Trade

Keep an Eye on the Volume

- Buying Volume
- Selling Volume
- High Volume
- Pullbacks

Analyze Your Position

High Liquidity and Volatility

Financial Services

Social Media Stocks

Chapter 5: Psychology and Mindset of a Successful Day Trader

Importance of a Positive Mindset

Shape up Your Trader's Mindset

Learn! Learn! Learn!

The Mindset of a Successful Trader

- Psychological Issues

- Create Discipline
- Patience
- Ways to Acquire a Trader Mindset
- How to Achieve Emotional Stability

Chapter 6: An Overview of Proven Day Trading Strategies

- High-frequency Trading (HFT)
  - Penny Stocks
- Momentum Trading

Chapter 7: Step-By-Step to a Successful Trade

- Building a Watchlist
- Introduction to Candlesticks
  - Long vs. Short
  - Marubozu
  - Long vs Short Shadows
  - Spinning Tops
  - Doji
  - Miscellaneous Info
  - Hammer and Hanging Man
- Exit Strategy
  - Support and Resistance
- Moving Average Trailing Stops

Volatility

Chapter 8: Understanding Trading Orders

Market Order

Limit Order

Stop-order

Stock-limit Order

Trailing Stop Order

Market-If-Touched Orders

Limit-If-Touched (LIT) Orders

How to Place an Order?

- Buy Orders
- Sell Orders
- Order Execution
- Contract Notes

Chapter 9: Strategies to Minimize Risk While Trading

Plan Trades

The One-Percent Rule

Set Stop-loss

Diversification

Reward-Risk Ratio

Avoid Volatile Conditions

A Higher Timeframe
Forex Risk Management
Limit Leverage
Conclusion
References

© **Copyright 2019 by** _____ -
All rights reserved.

This document is geared towards providing exact and reliable information in regard to the topic and issue covered. The publication is sold with the idea that the publisher is not required to render accounting, officially permitted, or otherwise, qualified services. If advice is necessary, legal or professional, a practiced individual in the profession should be ordered.

- From a Declaration of Principles which was accepted and approved equally by a Committee of the American Bar Association and a Committee of Publishers and Associations.

In no way is it legal to reproduce, duplicate, or transmit any part of this document in either electronic means or in printed format. Recording of this publication is strictly prohibited and any storage of this document is not allowed unless with written permission from the publisher. All rights reserved.

The information provided herein is stated to be truthful and consistent, in that any liability, in terms of inattention or otherwise, by any usage or abuse of any policies, processes, or directions contained within is the solitary and utter responsibility of the recipient reader. Under no circumstances will any legal responsibility or blame be held against the publisher for any reparation, damages, or monetary loss due to the information herein, either directly or indirectly.

Respective authors own all copyrights not held by the publisher.

The information herein is offered for informational purposes solely, and is universal as so. The presentation of the information is without contract or any type of guarantee assurance.

The trademarks that are used are without any consent, and the publication of the trademark is without permission or backing by the trademark owner. All trademarks and brands within this book are for clarifying purposes only and are the owned by the owners themselves, not affiliated with this document.

Introduction

There is a popular belief that no magical spell exists by which you can conjure success in life. Success is the perfect combination of focus, commitment, hard work, knowledge, persistence, and sheer will. Similarly, success in the stock market as a day trader is based on investment at the right time in the right stock or currency. That's how you move up the success ladder. You cannot learn overnight the winning tactics of the stock market. It is more about ironing out the kinks in your strategy by reading and digesting the right content from a good book.

This book will equip you with the knowledge you need for succeeding in the stock market. The stock market is a different world. No matter how big your capital is, there always is a bigger capital afloat in the market, ready to feed on yours. So, amidst all the Wall Street giants, do you stand a chance when you confront them? Or do they stand a chance when they come face to face with you? By the time you have turned the last leaf of the book, your trading arsenal will be full of weapons that will give you the power to not only survive but thrive as a day trader. This book is for all those who have a fire in their hearts to win in the teeth of fierce competition. Winners have a habit of getting stronger when they land in hot competition. With the right knowledge and skills that you can find in this book, you can be able to outcompete other contenders.

You will learn in this book the art of reading the candlestick chart. I will explain different types of candlesticks in words and visual examples. I have added in this book in-depth explanations on dojis, white and black candlesticks, hammers, hanging man, the evening star, and the morning star and other types of candlesticks. As dojis should be studied in the form of patterns, I will explain it concerning the preceding and succeeding candlestick patterns. With the inclusion of candlestick charts along with other important topics, this book has become a complete package for those who are about to begin their career in day trading. I encourage you to take a notebook and jot down the tricks that you find useful in the book to use them when you are preparing your day trading strategy.

Day trading or active trading centers around buying and selling of stocks over a single trading day. This type of trading has exploded into popularity over the past decade. Savvy traders can rake in a big amount of money through day trading. Stock prices have also gone ballistic. There is a big number of companies that are getting listed on the stock market each week. Many people think that the stock market is all about buying a stock and then holding your position for a while to make a profit. However, the stock market is much more than a single buy and hold technique. There are lots of factors that you need to consider before you pull up your socks to enter the realm of day trading. You need to make sure that you have loaded up your arsenal with all the traditional and modern weapons to create a winning situation for you in the stock market.

In this book, I will explain the fundamentals of day trading and how this technique is different from the other styles of trading and investing. The book is divided into several chapters, each explaining a certain aspect of day trading. Let's see what each chapter of the book has got for you.

The first chapter of the book focuses on the basic concepts of day trading. I will explain what day trading is and how it works. You will learn about the difference between day trading and swing trading. I will then move on to explaining the difference between day trading and long term investing. You will learn about the basic concepts and the pros and cons of each type of trading. The chapter ends on giving you an account of the benefits of day trading and the disadvantages of day trading. After reading this chapter, you will be able to enter the world of stocks with a clear mind.

The second chapter of the book focuses on the do's and don'ts of day trading. I recommend that you keep a diary or a notebook with you while you read this book so that you can note the important points. The things that you are allowed to do and the things that you must not do in day trading should be in your short term working memory all the time if you want to be successful as a day trader.

The third chapter of the book carries the main tools of day trading. In the first section, I will give a list of the tools and their distinct features. The importance of a trading community will also come under discussion in this chapter.

The fourth chapter of the book focuses on choosing the right stock in the stock market. This chapter is highly important. Whether you will win or lose in a position is decided at the moment you choose a stock to trade. Some people randomly enter a position thinking that they can benefit from the fluctuation in the price of the stock. This is not the right thing to do. There are many factors such as the volume of the stock, the level of liquidity and volatility in the stock, and the nature of stocks. I will also explain some hotshot stocks that have been the focus of big traders for a while.

The fifth chapter of the book is the most important as well. It deals with unearthing the right mindset that a day trader must-have. Day trading is not for all types of mindsets. If you are an aspiring day trader, you should study this chapter in detail to know what it takes to be a day trader. Unless you have the right mindset, you cannot succeed. You must be willing to educate yourself, control your emotions, be patient, and be disciplined if you want to build a fortune out of day trading. I have included in this chapter the key techniques which you can practice to build a trader's mindset.

The sixth chapter of the book deals will walk you through a set of proven day trading techniques and strategies. I will explain the concept of High-frequency Trading also known as HFT. Then I will move on to explaining the concept of penny stocks and momentum trading.

The seventh chapter of the book is about building a plan to execute a successful trade. This includes building a watchlist of stocks that you must monitor and buy when they are ripe for investment. I will explain the method to build the watchlist. Next comes building an effective exit strategy in the market. Other topics that will come under discussion are support and resistance levels and volatility-based trading approaches. I will unveil how volatility is not always a viable option for stock investing.

The second last chapter of the book revolves around understanding the trading orders. This is the practical phase of the book. You can open up your electronic trading platform and start practicing in a demo account that I tell you. In the first section of this chapter, I will shed light on different types of orders that you can place in the market. Market orders, limit orders, stop orders, stop-limit orders are among the many types of orders that I will discuss in this section. Each type of order has its importance. Some orders help you minimize your losses in the market while other orders help you raise the scale of your profits. In the second section of the book, I will explain how you can place an order on a trading platform. It contains details of the buy and sells orders.

The last chapter of the book focuses on several strategies that you need to minimize the risks that are involved in day trading. You will get to know how you can avoid these risks. One way is to diversify your portfolio. The chapter ends on educating the readers on the ways to limit risks in Forex trading. This includes limiting your leverage that becomes kryptonite of most traders.

Chapter 1: The Basic Concepts of Day Trading

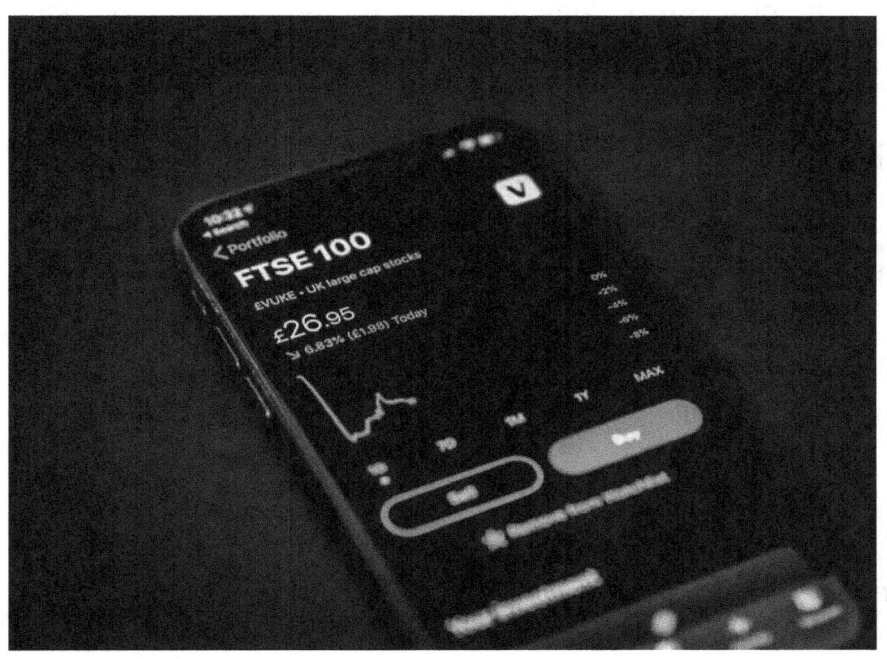

If you have chosen to buy this book, you may already have been intrigued by the exciting personal and financial rewards that day trading possesses. If you are interested in day trading, you might possibly have heard about the amazing and fascinating tales of some big monetary benefits that day trading brought for some investors or you might simply want to change your daily routine by switching it from an active job to working from home.

At the same time, you might have heard about the notorious stock market crashes and some horror stories about how people lost big sums of money. These thoughts might have compelled you to think twice whether day trading would suit you as a profession. In this chapter, I will try to address these critical questions by explaining what day trading is and how it works. I will also explain the difference among day trading and swing trading and long term investing. I will also walk you through the benefits and the downsides of day trading.

What Is Day Trading?

Day trading refers to the transactions that are performed by traders on financial securities within a restricted period of a single trading day. Simply put, it is the buying and selling of different types of securities in a short and limited time frame. It is pertinent to mention here that day trading is be limited to stocks only, and it encompasses futures and currencies as well. The basic point to feed in mind is that day trading spans over a single day. You cannot roll over the open trade positions overnight to the next day. There was a time once when the only people who could actively take part in trade were the ones who belonged to large financial institutions, trading houses, and brokerages. However, things have considerably changed since the advent of the internet. Now there are online trading houses and brokers which made it possible for an average investor to actively trade.

Day trading is a lucrative career if you understand its basics and execute it properly. It is a fact that it can be a little challenging for the people who are new to it and are not well-prepared or they don't have a well-planned strategy to win the game. The key is to understand the fact that even seasoned day traders can certainly hit some rough patches in business and experience painful losses. All days are not hay days.

You need to understand the fact that day trading is about profiting off changes in the price of an asset. There are a variety of strategies and techniques that you can use to capitalize on the inefficiencies of markets. It should also be kept in mind that day trading is characterized by in-depth technical analysis and it also requires objectivity and self-discipline.

How Day Trading Works?

The basic thing about day trading is that it is not like an ordinary investing technique. Investing is the technique of buying a bunch of stakes in a particular asset that would build a profit for you over the long term. How long it takes varies from investment to investment, but it may span over years. Investors do in-depth research on a stock and remain greatly concerned about the crests and troughs of the stocks they are investing in. They look out for the companies which tend to make big profits, which avoid debts, which pay them off on time if they accumulate them, which keep a powerful line of products, and which escape from litigation.

On the other hand, day trading focuses on buying securities and selling them in a single day. It is common for day traders to use borrowed money to take advantage of little fluctuations in prices of liquid stocks. Day traders use the same wisdom as a long-term investor does as they too buy at a low price and sell at a higher price. The only difference is the length of timeframe.

Day traders work in a compressed window of time. Let's assume that a day trader buys 500 shares of a stock at 9 am. After half an hour, the price for the stock begins to rise and the day trader sells the stock. If the stock has a rise in price by $0.50 per share, the day trader will bag $250 minus commission.

Day trading is common in stock markets and foreign exchange (Forex) markets. Day traders usually are well-educated and also well-funded. They have big leverages to trade and also have short-term trading techniques and strategies up their sleeves to capitalize on small fluctuations in prices of liquid currencies or stocks. Day traders have to be vigilant about small events that cause slight movements in the prices of stocks. The best technique is to trade the news. Prices of liquid stocks move on big and small news announcements such as corporate earnings, economic statistics, and fixing of interest rates. Markets rapidly react to this news.

Some day traders use the scalping technique which aims at making small profits by following little price changes throughout the day. Range trading is also popular among day traders as it employs support and resistance techniques to determine decisions about buying and selling. As already mentioned, there is the third technique known as news-based trading. Traders benefit from the volatility that originates due to different pieces of news. Another technique is known as high-frequency trading (HFT) in which a trader uses algorithms to exploit inefficiencies in the markets.

Day Trading vs. Swing Trading

Swing trading refers to the practice of making a profit from the swings in the market happening from over a day to over a week. Day traders are in and out of the market for over a day. Swing traders tend to stay longer in the market. They can hold multiple positions in the market for several months. I would say that swing traders fall in between day traders and trend traders when it comes to the period involved in trading. In trend trading, traders get gains by analyzing the momentum of an asset in a specific direction. They enter into longer positions when a trend is set in the upward direction.

Swing trading offers plenty of opportunities for traders. Its dollar risk per trade is not as much higher as compared to trend trading, because there are closer stops. It also provides a greater profit-making opportunity on single trades as compared to day trading. The quick and hefty rewards offer greater emotional satisfaction to the trader. There is a downside that you have to work hard on almost all the time to manage your trades, which is that it is highly likely you miss out on some big moves over the course of the hold period by which you can make big profits. Also, frequent trading cost much in terms of higher commission costs.

As a day trader, you should look out for the stocks that keep moving predictably. Swing trading is different from day trading in the sense that in this type of trading you need to hold your stocks over a longer period. It is a different style of trading and you have to use a different toolkit to succeed in that.

Day trading attracts the traders who lookout for fast compounding of profit returns. If a trader risks 0.5% of the capital and lose, he will lose the same amount which is 0.5%, but if he wins, he will make 1%. If he executes six trades a day, he will add around 1.5% to his balance with lesser trading fees. A 1% per day average would grow his trading account by over 200% over the entirety of a year. But it is not that much easy as it appears to be. You can get some real fast gains but you also can wash out your trading account through day trading if you are prone to making hasty decisions.

On the other hand, swing trading is slower than day trading. You bag gains and post losses slowly. Still, you keep the option of doing swift trades that can result in some big gains and losses. If a swing trader risks 0.5% of his capital on each trade to bag 1% to 2% profit and earns 1.5% on average, he would lose 0.5% on the lost trading positions. If he executes six trades a day and wins 50% of them, he will be able to add 3% to his trading account balance with lesser fees to pay. So, over a year that's an increase of 36%. It sounds more concrete and stable but it offers lesser potential to earn than that of day trading.

There is a norm in the world of stock trading that traders do day trading and swing trading at the same time. I also do both. I am always aware of the fact that I am managing two different businesses, and that they have different methods, techniques, and they demand a different approach from me. If you have made up your mind to keep the two running side by side, you should make sure that you have adopted the right approach for picking up stocks. I have made it a rule not to do both types of trading for the same stocks. Swing traders look out for the stocks of healthy and strong companies that won't lose their worth overnight. On the other hand, you can take that risk while you are day trading. Even if a company is bound to go bankrupt, you can go for it and make short term profits during the day. There are lots of stocks in which people day trade and make profits but lose their capital when they choose to hold the stock overnight. Choose the stocks wisely for day trading and swing trading.

Let us assume you have bought a stock and have also kept it for a week. It is time to sell now but you are not making any profit as the price is too low. As a swing trader, you can defer the sale and hold the stock for another day or a week so that the price may recover. That's not the case in day trading. You must sell the stock even if you have to sell it for a loss to make sure that you are not holding the same overnight.

Buy Long Sell Short

Day traders buy stocks in the hope that the price will jump during the day. This technique is known as buying long. If the prices are dropping, there is another technique that you can use. You can always sell short and make big profits. You can borrow some shares from the broker and then sell them in the hope that the price will drop and you can buy the same shares at a lower price and make a profit. The technique is known as short selling. In short selling, traders expect the prices to go down.

Suppose you have bought 100 shares of Microsoft and sold them for $100 per share. The share price falls below $90 and you buy back the same 100 shares that you had sold earlier on, and return it to the broker. You have bagged the profit of $10 per share, which means you have made $1,000 by short selling. If the price takes a U-turn and rises above $100 to $110 per share, you still have to sell it to the broker. In that case, you will incur a loss of $1,000.

Day Trading vs. Long Term Investing

Day trading and long-term investing are considered viable forms of trading in securities. Lots of traders opt to do both. Day trading involves trades that usually last for seconds to minutes while long term investing involves trades that remain open for several months and even years. You have to buy and then hold for a lengthy period. There is no room for quick decisions.

Day trading and long-term investing differ regarding the requirement of the capital involved in the process, the level of skills required, and the commitments needed to perform the job. Day trading and long-term investments are key parts of a well-managed and diversified strategy. Both offer you a passive form of income and great sources for the generation of wealth.

If you are in the United States of America, you will need $25,000 min to open a brokerage account for day trading. There is no minimum capital requirement to do day trading in the currency market, but the recommended amount is $1,000. If you are aiming at day-trading in futures, the best amount to start with is $5,000 to 7,500. A long-term investment is usually aimed at the stock market where the level of unpredictability and liquidity is lower than the currency market. Futures expire after a fixed date therefore they are not ideal for long term investment.

Investing for the long term involves significant research into the company in which you are injecting your money. Long term investment can be done even if you are doing an active day job. When you have got the desired capital, you should spend a couple of hours each day on the stocks that you have got on your radar for investment. The key part of long-term investment, as opposed to day trading, is the amount of research that you must put in before you buy the stocks.

The research time differs from person to person. Some people opt to be more active and consume lots of hours watching the stock movement and reading research reports while others spend just a couple of hours on research and decide which way they need to go (Mitchell, 2018).

Benefits of Day Trading

Day trading is the type of profession that you can tailor yourself. You can customize it as per your needs. You can either pair it up with your current job or you can adopt it as a full-time profession. The point is that you can work when and where you want if you opt to be a day trader. You get the freedom to structure your day as you need, and you can work from home or even when you are traveling.

It is a small business and it doesn't need a big amount of investment to get started. The initial investment in the equipment that is a computer, a couple of monitors, a fast and reliable internet connection, and trading software. They are relatively inexpensive. You can live anywhere and do your work. You can move to Florida, Maine, and Bangor, and still, be able to do your business. If you have a burning desire to go mountaineering in summers, you can pack up and go without worrying about loss of income or job. You can trade from the heights of the mountains. It doesn't mean that you compromise your vacations for work by doing trading while camping. The fact is that most people cannot even go on a vacation because they are too busy at work. This profession allows you to pair up vacation fun and work.

As an active trader, you have no commitments of any kind to anyone. You work as an independent person hence you answer to no one except yourself. You don't have a nasty boss who is always glaring from his cabin to check if you are working or not. When you are ill, you have the liberty to stay in bed for the day. You can wear comfortable clothes. There is no need to wear a tie that almost chokes you. There also is no need to wear high heels that can dislocate your heels or back. A T-shirt, duck slippers and shorts are all that you need.

The best thing about day trading is that you get to develop your style that is compatible with your nature, your disposition, and is easy-going. When the market appears to be too volatile to handle, you can take the day off and do the pending tasks such as household repair, cooking, or visiting a family member or a friend. You can play with your kids, run errands, or go shopping with the money that you have saved by keeping out of a tricky market.

The top upside about choosing day trading as a field of earning money is that you don't need a degree or a specialized level of skills for the purpose. You will have to absorb plenty of knowledge before you could declare yourself fit for active trading, but you don't have to get some kind of certification in this field. The internet is loaded with several free resources that can help you upgrade your knowledge base in the field of investing. You can enroll in them. The best approach is to pair up the study of online resources with the study of a good book. While you have to manually search for different topics on the internet, a good book offers you multiple topics in a single place that too with in-depth explanation and examples. Once you have scanned the basics, you can move on to buying a trading software that would further keep you updated with the latest trading news, charts, and information about different stocks. Never try to dig into the trading software from the beginning. This can be a mistake that can put you on the hook. Solidify your knowledge at the start and then gradually move on to the next level. Many websites offer aspiring day traders an opportunity to practice trading on demo software. This facility comes for free or for a small fee.

Another best thing about day trading is that you get the chance to be your boss. You work from the comforts of your home, sipping your coffee. You don't need to seek permission from any higher authority to execute your trades. You are responsible for profits and accountable for however the trade goes on.

One of the top advantages of being a day trader is that you get to sleep peacefully. All of your trades close when the day ends. There is no risk of an overnight loss. There is no risk that your stock value will drop to zero while you are lost in the valley of dreams. Day trading offers you the security of your profit and greater control over your trading business. If it went well during the day and you bagged sufficient profits, you can go to sleep soundly overnight.

Even if the market is taking a bad turn, you can take advantage of that. While it struggles, you can short sell and bag profits while it dips to the bottom. If you can make money off bearish conditions in the stock market, you get a competitive advantage over traders. Long term investors have to focus on the fundamentals of a company like its overall health, information about who is in the management board and how they are running the company, the past reports about the company, the record of the profits it posted, its contracts with government and non-government agencies, its tradition of awarding dividends to shareholders and its financial statements. So, that's quite a lot of work. On the other hand, day traders just have to focus on the technical analysis throughout the day to make successful deals. They just need to run through the current analysis, make transactions, and get profits. You will only be concerned about the present moment. Take note of the current price, the current volume, and the level of volatility in the price of the particular stock (Stock Market Day Trading, n.d).

Downsides of Day Trading

All that I have discussed above is good news, and you might be very happy to read that. As there are thorns with roses, and deadly lightning with rain, there are some flipsides of day trading as well. My aim to state the downsides of day trading is not to discourage you and cool off your determination but to motivate you to keep a check on whatever you do during business hours. When you know about the downsides, you will be able to save yourself from pitfalls. These are just realities that a day trader must know. When I started trading at first, I spent a considerable time on knowing what bad can happen to me. The trading route is littered with lots of bumps. Some expert investors considered it just short of war. There is a war of profits and losses. This business crushes people more than any other business does. There is a belief that about 80% of those who try this quit soon. They lose their trading balance by ignorance or by taking foolish risks or just by trading too much. Some of them even cannot handle the stress.

If the rewards are high, so are tradeoffs. The stock market can be a ruthless arena on occasions. Just like any other knowledge field and a business venture, day trading demands proficiency and a combination of skills because it gets superfast sometimes. You have to do multitasking to keep up with the pace of the market, which puts many traders at a disadvantage in the open market trade.

As I have mentioned, day trading demands decision-making in a split-second. It does suit the people who tend to be slow in making decisions. If you aim to be a successful trader, you need to analyze this market quickly. When you are presented with a high-probability trade opportunity, you should act fast with confidence. At the same time, you should be able to manage your trade and maintain discipline so that you can manage your rewards and risk equally well.

For some of you, day trading can be boring. While the market moves at a lightning speed, you have to make quick decisions, which takes a toll on your emotions. You also have to deal with surging emotions of greed and fear. You must check them before they get over your brain and guide your actions. The most challenging part while you do all this stuff is sitting before a computer screen for hours. All you have to do is to watch the market and do nothing else. For the majority of the time, the market will move without providing you an opportunity to bag profits. This can be boring sometimes. Therefore, you must train yourself to sit calmly and wait before an opportunity knocks your doors.

Chapter 2: The Dos and Don'ts of Day Trading

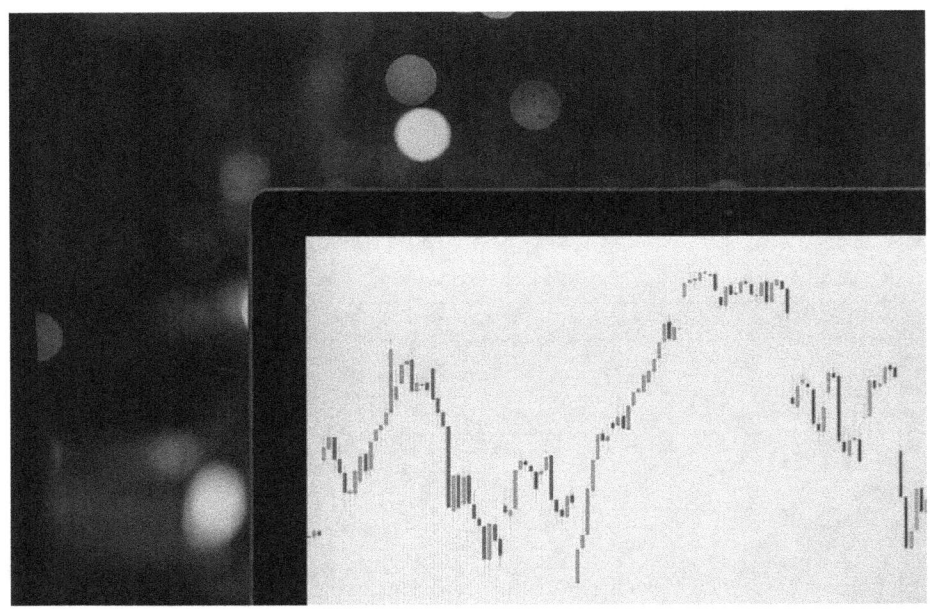

Day trading is a business that you can set up fast. The very first step is to define if you are a full-time or part-time day trader. In this chapter, I will explain the basic tips for day traders. I will shed light on what kind of weapons you are going to need along the way. I assume that you have allocated the budget that you want to invest in your trading business. The first rule of a trading business is that you should not trade with the money that, if lost, is likely to dent your lifestyle. This money, in the world of trading, is known as 'scarred money.' When you are trading with scarred money, fear comes to haunt your decisions and you lose more often a winning bet. Don't let fear color your business decisions. If you do that, you will be making the worst possible trading choices and lose money in the end. If you get the chance to interview traders and brokers, you will realize this fact.

The next rule is connected to the first one, which is that you should only use the money in a trade that you can afford to lose. Newbie traders lose money. I know lots of traders who have washed away their entire accounts. Some of them lose their cars, houses, furniture, etc. If you cannot afford to lose the money that you have invested, you should not invest at all. Better postpone your trading career for a while until you have accumulated more cash that you can spare solely for trading.

Basic Day Trading Tips

Day trading focuses on buying and selling stock during the same day that's why the techniques and tips are different for this type of trading from the other types. A successful day trader is the one who can take advantage of little movements in the prices of stock by playing around them in the right way. This game may appear to be dangerous for the newbie traders who generally don't like to adhere to a well-formulated strategy.

Day trading demands that you gain sufficient knowledge about the stocks that you want to buy. As already mentioned and suggested, day traders need to keep themselves up-to-date with the latest knowledge of events of news happening around. This includes the general economic outlook and the Fed's interest rate plans. For example, when the COVID-19, a deadly virus, hit hard at the global economy at the start of 2020, the world markets started panicking. Dow Jones fell flat more than once. The oil market crashed because the global food supply chain, trade chain, and flight pattern got disturbed. Financial markets started reeling from the economic halt. Industries stopped working and cargo ships docked for an unlimited time. All these factors accounted for the fall in the global financial markets, especially the oil market. Amidst this chaos, the Kingdom of Saudi Arabia (KSA) and Russia were caught up in a price war regarding the sale of oil. This further pushed oil to the downside. Suddenly, the oil market rose and made significant gains. The day traders who were aware of the news about US President Donald Trump's mediation between KSA and Russia bagged a significant amount of profits by buying early and selling when it touched its peak.

Another important thing is the rise in the prices of gold as oil fell to the ground. Over the years it has become a tradition that whenever oil faces an uncertain future and the global markets react to panic across the world, gold strengthens its position. Day traders who carefully watch the markets and make an in-depth study of different commodities capitalize even on uncertain fluctuations in the markets. The takeaway is that you should do your homework. Better make a wish list of the stocks that you would like to trade-in and keep yourself aware of the latest news about those companies. Scan all the business news that comes your way by visiting reliable financial markets.

Day trading demands that you set aside plenty of time during the day. If you are prone to get carried away by distractions, you should reconsider your daily routines and habits. Don't take up this profession if you don't have sufficient time to spare. Day trading demands that the trader consumes sufficient time on tracking the markets and hunting down potential opportunities, which can pop up any time during the trading hours. The key is to move fast.

You are not supposed to gallop like a horse in the beginning. Instead try to focus on one or two stocks at maximum during one season as tracking them will be easier. You can choose to buy fractional shares at the start just to get the taste as to how the markets will behave. If Apple shares are trading at $200, you can ask your broker to purchase $50 worth of it, which makes up the one-fourth of the total value of the share.

Don't trade in penny stocks. At the start, you might be looking for low prices and deals, but it is better to stay away from the penny stocks as much as you can. Their chances of hitting the jackpot are low. Many stocks trade under $5 per share and get de-listed from major stock exchanges. Unless you are sure that a real opportunity lies in your way, avoid buying them.

Stay realistic in your trading ventures. As you get into top gear in the world of trading, you should make sure that you don't miss out on some decent gains just because you behave greedily. Markets, at times, appear to be tricky therefore it is best to settle down for small profits rather than losing heavily by falling for greed. The key to a satisfying trading business is not to regret if you miss out on a potential profit-making opportunity. Markets, sometimes, behave in a tricky manner therefore it is in your best interest to be content on small profits. You can always have the chance to buy the same stock upon the next dip. Rest assured that the stock will rebound. Each small profitable deal will boost your confidence levels and offer you a chance to apply the strategy again.

If you are new to trading, you should know that trading on margins means that you are borrowing money from the brokerage firm to which you are registered. If you use margins appropriately, you can amplify the trading results. While you get excited about how much profits you can bag with the help of margins, you also should know the fact that the same is true for losses as well. If a particular trade goes against you, you will be posting some heavy losses. As a beginner, you need to stay in control of the amount you have invested. It is a better strategy to start without getting involved in margins.

Lots of orders that are placed by investors start executing when the market opens in the morning. This adds to volatility in the prices of commodities. A seasoned day trader will be able to recognize the patterns and pick the right profits at the right time, but as a beginner, it will be hard for you to analyze the patterns and understand them for profitmaking. It is better to let the market flow for 15 to 20 minutes before entering it. It settles down to a predictable pattern in a matter of time. The middle hours of the market usually are less volatile than the morning and the evening hours. Start by trading in this window.

Day trading can turn out to be pretty risky and there is a higher chance of loss if you don't adhere to the advice of seasoned traders. You can end up posting significant losses in a no time therefore it is recommended that you set aside some funds that you can trade with in the wake of loss. This money should be in addition to the money that you keep aside for your living expenses. This ensures that your risk quotient is lower and that you are not putting everything at stake. This also adds to your satisfaction as well.

One interesting tip is to limit your orders. When you place an order in the open market, it is executed at the fixed time at the best price available for that order. There is not a price guarantee for that. You should limit orders and it would help you trade with higher precision in uncertain times. Beginners often fall for unreliable sources of information such as SMS, emails, advertisements, and mails, which make claims about above-normal profits. I don't rubbish all the claims as bogus, but the fact is that you should do proper authentication for your transactions. Don't trust a random source of information.

Day trading will test you emotionally, psychologically, and financially. You need to stay calm and deal with each situation as calmly and smoothly as you can. Day trading demands from your discipline, time, and skills. It is not the skill that you can develop overnight. These tips can help you get started with day trading. Self-learning is always the best way to learn when it comes to day trading. In the next section, I will explain the do's and don'ts of day trading that a beginner day trader must adhere to for a successful career (Bajpai, 2019).

The Do's of Day Trading Business

Here is a rundown of the things that you must do when you enter day trading business.

• The basic thing is to be persistent in your approach. You should keep going even amid adversity. Just think of the last time you have learned something worthwhile or fun. Remember how you behaved when you started playing baseball or fishing. Did you become a master the very first time you did that? Did you behave awkwardly or were you smooth in handling the equipment? Did the bat drop from your hands? Can you recall a person who mastered it the first time? Even if there is anyone, he would be one out of thousands. No one masters anything from the first attempt. You need time to build and polish your skills. You usually are pretty bad at first but you learn to make it right over time because you have an urge buried down in your heart to make it better. If you are desperate to become a musician, you will become one someday. Same is the case with day trading. It can be frustrating at the start. Don't try to give up on a couple of failed trades. You may lose some part of your capital while you desperately attempt to bag profits from a trade. If you have failed, you must push past this pain and keep your gaze fixed at the horizon. You must keep in mind the final destination. Only then you can get over the desperation and the frustration.

- When you make up your mind about making a career out of day trading, you should create a tangible and practical plan that you must strictly follow. Every business demands a strategic plan that you must build and evolve along the way. A good plan should contain all aspects of your trading strategy. Without a solid plan, you are not trading but gambling. So, don't just gamble. Follow set rules. Your plan may contain the timing of your trade, the amount of initial investment, the companies you want to invest in, the timing you want to hold a stock, and the time you will have to invest in studying technical reports, charts, and volumes of a given stock.

- Do prepare a checklist. A checklist usually is as much important as a trading plan. You need to include your trading rules in the list. You should be satisfied with the checklist before you enter a trade. For example, you can decide how much leverage you need to take and what should be the risk-reward ratio. Going through the checklist each time you make a new trade cuts down your chance of making any kind of silly beginner-level mistakes. Once you have done trading for a couple of months, all the points of the checklist will be fed in your brain, and you will not need them anymore.

- The next thing you should do is to follow a strict routine. Day trading is not like a job or physical business that binds you for a set period. Trading is a lonely endeavor and some of you may struggle after finding themselves in a new situation in which they are not under the watch of any kind and they are not being instructed on what to do. It is you who have to make decisions and shape your future. Therefore, you must have a routine. It will be risky for your capital and your business if you take long breaks from work during active hours of trading. You may miss out on high-probability opportunities. If you have set up a daily routine by clearly defining your goals, you can remain on track and build a successful career as an independent trader.

- If at any point you feel that you don't have sufficient learning, you should take time to learn. There is always room for that no matter how much you think you have studied books and online material. You can lose all your money in a matter of hours. The best learning approach is to learn the jargon at first and understand the basic concepts. You must know what a particular word means. Just think of an engineer! Can you call a person an engineer if he or she doesn't know what a particular word in the book of engineering means? What will you do if he has not attended the college of engineering but call himself an engineer? Would you trust him? Would you like them to build a bridge in your hometown? Would you like them to work on the flyover in your city? You will do everything a bit to keep them away from these projects. You will not hand over your house construction project to an engineer who has just graduated. You will find someone with lots of experience and knowledge. Similarly, you should do that the same when you start trading. Consider yourself as a novice engineer who knows a little and who also has little experience to his credit. When you have traded for a while, you will be able to develop a knowledge base that you can use to gain more knowledge such as to learn better and faster. Apply these initial concepts to your trading practices and improve your knowledge.

- Never at any point should you think that you are expert enough to drop the need for detailed homework. Many a time it happens that a person when gains sufficient experience or knowledge starts feeling proud and superior. This false sense of superiority clouds his judgment and he bitterly fails at a point so badly that he ruins himself and others as well. Always do your homework before each trade. Doing your homework means that you are researching all aspects of your daily trade. It includes proper analysis of a bunch of companies you will select for day trading, the products they offer, and financial events and their effects on market sentiment. You can find lots of analysis in a cooked form on multiple platforms, but until you can derive your data, you cannot taste true success. The powerful rise in demand has given room to the rise of a breed of analysts that keep cooking analysis all day. You should pay heed to what they say but you also should do your math. Investigate the rise and fall of stocks and try to understand the factors that triggered a particular sentiment in the market. Listen to these analysts but follow their advice with great caution. If you blindly follow their advice, you may not be able to understand the reason behind your loss. Make conscious choices.

The Don'ts of Day Trading

Just like the do's, there are some don'ts of day trading as well. Here is a rundown of the things that you don't have to do if you want to survive in this business.

• The very first don't of day trading is emotional instability. If you feel that you lose emotional control easily and if you get angry or overly happy each time you try to make money, you are not following the recipe to success. A forex trader or stock trader cannot be angry or extremely happy. The best traders across the world are the ones who can part their emotions from trading. As a human, emotions are our weaknesses. We make mistakes when we get emotional. Don't let emotions carry you away and have greater control over what you buy and sell. It happens often when you make a big profit from a sale, you get happy and make a purchase that is triggered by euphoria rather than logic. It can wipe out the gains from your previous trade.

• If a person pays heed to rumors around him, the best method to deal with him is to ignore him. You will not like to talk to someone who always lends his ear to rumors about politics or other national issues. The same is true in the world of trading as well. You cannot listen to rumors and act on them. Well, it gets tempting to do so sometimes. Some scenarios fan rumors. For example, you are most likely to believe and act on rumors if you have invested a big amount in a particular stock and have not yet earned anything since morning and are desperate to earn before the day ends. You may feel tempted to heed to rumors if you have recently bagged profit by acting on a rumor. Your brain might convince you to repeat the practice again. Remember that you don't need to listen to rumors no matter whatever the scenario is. You must do in-depth research before you act on a rumor. You might have a friend who claims to be a master of trading and who has made lots of money and who is always ready to offer his advice, but it is not wise to always act on what he says. Your financial situation is always different from the situation of your friend. His trading strategy might be different. His capital might be bigger or smaller than yours. You don't always know what his stop-loss is or what his target price at which he would sell is. If he listens to a rumor and you follow suit, both of you will land in serious trouble. Similarly, don't always pay heed to what your broker says to you.

- The second don't that you must remember is that you should not isolate yourself from others. It is very natural for you to do so because it is the need of this business. There are two reasons as to why isolation happens in the first place. Day traders have to work from home and keep the focus on the latest analysis coming from different sources. The concentration and amount of study involved in it demand that you work in isolation. But is it healthy for you and your business? Isolation will take a toll on your mental and physical health hence there is a need to create joint working opportunities. Try to focus on teaming up with a group of professional traders who will provide each other support throughout the busy day. In this way, you will be able to get a sense of how other traders are approaching their business and how they are solving the problems that arise over the day. You will have the opportunity to collaborate and communicate amidst work, which will allow you to pick a bunch of tips. You will also be able to share your own experience with others. The last sentence may sound counterintuitive to you but the fact of the world remains that the more you give away, the more you receive. Your brain might have started telling you that you never trade your secrets, but that's half true. The things that have worked for you may not work for others because it is not only knowledge that matters in success but the conviction, the commitment, the focus, and the courage you pour in it that does the magic. Take it in the sense that when you create a culture of sharing, you invite others to share their thoughts as well. In this way, all members of a group can learn and grow.

- Don't fall for greed. Many day traders fail because they fall too easily for greed. Volatility in the market is bound to happen, and the best way to deal with it is to remain in control of yourself. As you get consistent in profitable trades, you start buying stocks in high volumes, which increases your risk of loss. I told you at the start that you should make it a rule that you will remain calm and steady while you trade. If you break that rule and try to enter a volatile market just because you have bagged a big profit recently, you are raising your chances of getting stuck and losing the profits and also a chunk of your capital. This may happen at the end of the day when the market gets volatile as many day traders close their deals. The temptation to enter the market shoots up. Just stay steady. Wait and watch the market for a while before you make a move (Maybury, 2016).

Chapter 3: The Main Tools of Day Trading

Just like any other business, day trading also requires a bunch of tools. You need a broker and a reliable trading platform to kick off your journey. Some of the required tools you may already have. Currently, trading has gone electronic and many traders have access to financial markets across the world through the internet. It is always a good idea to keep a telephone in case you need to talk to your broker. You will also need a computer and a laptop. In this chapter, I will explain detail about what kind of tools you need for the journey and why they are important.

The Tools

The basic tool is your computer. Technology is changing in a fast manner that's why you should make sure that you have a computer that has sufficient memory and a really fast processor that doesn't lag constantly or crash in the middle of the work. Most of the trading software require fast processors that can wrap up tasks rapidly. The second most important tool is the software you use. Most brokers offer a variety of software options that you can use. This software has the basic job of monitoring the prices of financial assets. Day traders usually want to use the software that would allow them to use different charts like timed charts and tick charts.

Ninja Trader is a popular software that you can use for charting and trading. Different brokerages are compatible with different software. The fact remains that you are going to need an awesome broker for your trading ventures. A good broker is your key to a profitable trade. With a bad broker, you can lose money. Many brokers are great and they have great software. Their price structures also are great. However, some are cheap as well. You should go through the online reviews before you select the broker for your investment ventures.

Remember that each broker will give you around three to six times leverage on your investment. If you invest around $30,000 in your trading account, you can have $120,000 buying power. That's a leverage of 4:1. In common trading language, leverage is called margin. You have full rights to trade on margins but you ought to be responsible about it. It is relatively easy to buy on the margins but is also easier to lose on the margins. If you lose, your broker takes the loss from the main capital you had invested in the account. That's the reason you should be in consultation with the trader over how much margin you should set. Margins can expose you to greater risks.

Margins work just as mortgage does for your house. You borrow a big amount of money and then buy your residence. Banks will give you a mortgage, but they won't take the responsibility or risk over the same. If you put $100,000 and borrow $900,000 from the bank on a mortgage, this makes a 10:1 leverage to buy a $1,000,000 house. If the price of the house jumps up to $1,200,000, you still owe the bank the original $900,000 and the interest. The profit you have made has come from the leverage that you were offered. You couldn't have bought the house if it were not for the leverage. If the price drops to $900,000, you owe the bank $900,000 and the interest. This drop in price has cost you $100,000, which means that you have lost all the original down payment. Keeping in view these situations, you should choose the broker that is well disciplined so that you should be given a margin call on each trade you make on leverage. A margin call is similar to a serious warning. Day traders must avoid receiving these margin calls. A margin call means that you must add more money to your account or else your broker will freeze your account.

The trading platform has the same amount of importance. Fast execution of trade is the key to a successful day trading career. Just imagine that you have to place orders in one minute and the trading platform hangs up for the next five minutes or the trading platform is too slow to load up in split second. If your broker doesn't have a fast software or trading platform that runs on hotkeys, you should think about changing the broker. You just simply cannot get the ins and outs of the trades in a faster way. When the stock's price spikes, you should be able to put money in your pocket by selling it real quick. You will not love to be fumbling to find your orders. Quick execution is the key here, which is why I recommend that you hire an efficient broker that focuses on and guarantees real fast trade execution.

The Trading Community

Trading is a tricky business. It is no easy feat and is not for the weak-hearted. You need to be emotionally strong as it can get emotionally overwhelming for you. Therefore, it is always the best way to join a trading community and ask them about their experiences. You can talk to them and learn about new methods of trading and strategies. You will have lots of alerts and hints about the stock market. You can chat in a private chat room with your close friends and family members as well. When I traded, I remained in communication with my friends on the telephone. We intimated each other about the possible fluctuations in the price. We also shared news reports, technical analysis, charts, and graphs via emails to keep our community up to date. This helped us save time. This also saved us from frustration as well that originated from lack of knowledge. Some trading platforms offer live chat service to traders as well.

If you join a general chat room, you can talk to experienced traders as well who would offer you the right advice on the base of experience. You can request them for tips and tricks of day trading. You can gradually work on growing your community or you can join an already established community. Creating and growing a community is free.

Online Trading Tools

All depending upon the instruments that you need and your level of experience, there are some tools that you can access online and use to make your trading business popular.

Tradingview

This is one of the top popular charting platforms that you can access online and use for giving a lift to your trading business. It generally covers all markets across the world such as indices, forex, stocks, and futures, etc. This program allows you to program a personalized script. It also offers you a variety of indicators that allow you to share charts with the trading community you have developed or have joined. It is free to sign up on the platform. You also can take free membership which offers you advanced features.

Stockcharts

Stockcharts' team is the pioneer in stock trading. They have been around for quite a long time and they offer several charts such as Line, Point & Figure, Candlestick, Renko, and Ichimoku. The most interesting thing about this platform is that you can see the overall price performance of the stock over a particular period. For example, you can measure what was the percentage when it closed the last January. It also tells how much higher or lower it was from the current price.

MT4

If you are a forex trader, you might probably have heard about this famous platform. You or some of your friends have likely been using it already for doing business in Forex. Many brokerage firms offer CFDs instruments on MT4. The best thing about MT4 is the level of response that it offers to its users. There is almost zero lag time if you hop from one chart to another. If you are a swing or a position holder, you would love this platform.

Chapter 4: Choosing the Right Stock to Trade

You never know when the market will be in a dire shape or good shape. To capitalize on different types of markets, you need to find a stock that is reacting well to the market. If the market is in dire condition, you need to find the stock that is sliding toward a potential breakdown. You can sell it short at the right point and make big profits.

The stock market functions in a specific manner. Your stock can suddenly shift its direction and compels you to make extraordinary decisions, which is overall bad for your trading business. With so much electronic information at our fingerprints, it is quite easy to succumb to poor analysis. If you are applying too many of the chart tools to a particular stock index, you are pushing yourself into a corner. I will explain in this chapter different indicators that you must keep an eye on during day trading. Just keep it simple. If you get yourself entangled in plenty of information, you should immediately stop. You need to step back and take a look at the bigger picture. You should analyze what are the essentials? Are there more buyers than sellers for a particular stock? Is the stock going up? Are there more sellers than buyers? Is it likely to go down? If you can answer all these questions, you can be a good day trader in the long term.

Keep an Eye on the Volume

Volume, if you see in the charts, is usually displayed in the bar at the bottom of each chart. The bars show the number of shares that are traded. Volume is one of the top indicators of the momentum of a particular stock. It is one of the predictive tools that have no link to the price of a particular stock. This is really valuable information if you carefully view it and analyze it. Volume has an independent existence in the charts and graphs. You can take it as a second opinion on which direction a particular stock is about to take. The more you delve deeper into the interpretation of the signals that volume gives, the more knowledge you will have about the stock, and the more confident you will feel when you are about to invest in the market. Reading the volume of a particular stock is a skill that you can only add to your skillset over the course of time. You can grasp and use some basic signals and concepts but only experience can teach you how to see through the nuances of volume displays in the stock market.

The basic rule of reading volume of a particular stock is that when the volume expands, the price either soars or dips. When the volume shrinks, the price also goes down. When the volume of a particular stock tends to expand and the price does not, the situation is commonly referred to as price/volume divergence. You can expect that the price that has not budged yet is likely to shoot up in a short time on the back of volume expansion.

While you are day trading, you must master the skill of reading the volume of a particular stock for leverage. The term volume represents a particular number of units that are traded over a particular period. Traders usually consider it as a key metric because it allows them to know the level of liquidity of a certain asset. The volume also tells you how easy it is to enter and get out of a position. Volume analysis can help you choose the stocks in which you are looking forward to trading by finding out the connection between volume and prices. There are two primary elements that you need to take into consideration as part of volume analysis. These are as under.

Buying Volume

When the volume is rising, you will have sufficient and easy time to buy and sell a certain quantity of stock. This is because traders are opting to stay in the market and you can fulfill the second part of the trade which is selling the stock when the price rises above a certain position. You must understand how the stock market moves. The stock market moves up and down on the back of transactions. Each transaction in the stock market must have a seller and a buyer. If you desire to buy a stock, you must be able to find a seller who is willing to sell it to you. If you want to sell, you must have a buyer there willing to buy it from you.

If you are hearing from stockbrokers that the buyers are in control of the market, it means that price is being pushed higher by significant buying. Buyer volume happens in the stock market when traders buy stocks at the offer price. Simply put, if a trader offers stock at a higher price than he had purchased the stock, it shows that there are traders in the market who are willing to buy the stock. Buyer volume happens at the offer price of a stock.

Selling Volume

Sellers wield more control over the market when the prices are being pushed to the bottom. Seller volume happens at the bid price. The bid of a stock represents the top marketed price that buyers will offer. If someone is offering to sell a stock at the bid price, it means that the seller wants to get rid of the stock. This demonstrates the seller volume. You can see this volume at the bottom of the stock price chart. Charts usually depict trading volume in the form of vertical bars, with each bar displaying the number of shares that were traded in a particular window of time. If the volume bars on your chart are red, it means that the price has dropped during the trading window. If the volume is in the green bar, it means that the price rose and the market was driven by a hefty buyer volume.

Day traders love to gravitate toward a stock that has a high amount of trading volume or toward the stocks that has an extraordinarily higher volume on a particular day. If the volume floats lower than usual, it alludes to a diminishing interest in a particular stock on a certain day. It means that there will be lower price movements in the stock and that as a trader it will hard for you to get in and out of a position on that stock. Therefore, you should watch the flow of volume. Greater volume flow allows you to get in a position and move out of it as the price moves up.

High Volume

You need to pay attention to the days that start with higher-than-average volume. These days offer high volatility and a higher chance that prices will move either to the upside or to the downside. You can tell whether it will go down or up by analyzing if the volume is happening at the offer price or the bid price. A rise in volume shows that something is happening to the stock. There should be a trigger behind the rise such as a news release or a bunch of active traders who have panicked. Monitoring the trading volume of a stock can help you in carefully analyzing the price movements of the stock. If the volume is rising and so is the price, it hints on the eagerness of the buyers to buy a particular stock.

Pullbacks

Volume should be greater when the price moves upward, and it should be lower when the price slides against the trend, also known as pullbacks. This shows a powerful trajectory in the direction of the trend and weakness in pullbacks, making the trend likely to carry on. High volume with sharp movements in the price means that the trend is weakening or has been set to reversal. If you are witnessing a sudden spike in the volume of a stock, it may signal toward the end of a trend. A sudden spike in the volume can be five to ten times greater than the average volume for a stock. These are known as exhaustion moves and they happen when a sufficient amount of shares have changed hands and there is no one to push the price further in the direction of the trend. From this point, the price can quickly reverse to where it had started. So, it is riskier to enter a position at this point. Better stay out of the market and wait for the correction.

The volume offers plenty of information about a stock when you are day trading. You can use it to pick stocks that you need for day trading. Your day trading stocks must have more than average volume if you want to enter a position. This is how you can control risk as you can cut down on losses. You also can bag more profit as there is a handsome number of traders who will be willing to buy your stock. It should be kept in mind that just volume analysis is not the best way to consider buying a stock. It just offers supplemental information and it must be used in combination with other factors.

Analyse Your Position

Stocks, just like everything else in the financial world, should be well-tailored to your goals and your financial situation. There is no singular approach while you trade in stocks. You ought to analyze first how much wealth you have that you can invest in the stock market. Write down somewhere the total capital you have and the amount that you can put on the risk. The next step is to carry out a discount search in the market. The best way to do that is by studying the market and analyzing which sectors reflect your personal needs, values, and personality. Do it each day. Also, time yourself and make a head start right when the trading day opens.

As you are about to open your position, keep a check on your emotions. It is not a good habit to get emotionally attached to a particular stock. You have to analyze the patterns each day to find out what is the right time to enter the market and what is the right time to exit it after bagging profit or cutting down on losses.

The best method to choose a stock for day trading is by keeping touch with the latest news about the market. By staying in touch with the news I don't mean that you glue yourself to the television. Instead, it means that you should know when the earnings season of a stock gets close according to the economic calendar. This is how you can enter positions for the stocks that are likely to post profits in a couple of days. The best method to stay up to date is to keep a calendar in your home and tick mark the dates on which different companies are likely to post profits.

High Liquidity and Volatility

Liquidity, in the financial markets, refers to how fast an asset is bought or sold in the financial market. Liquidity also refers to how trading is going to affect the price of the security. Liquid stocks can be easily traded during the day and they also tend to be highly discounted as compared to other stocks, which makes them cheaper. Equity which is offered by organizations that have high market caps has higher liquidity than the corporations that have lower market caps. It is because it is way easier to find out sellers and buyers for the stock.

Financial Services

Usually, financial services stocks offer excellent stocks for day trading. Take the example of the Bank of America which is one of the top traded stocks as per shares traded in a single session. It also is a prime candidate that traders may choose for day trading because there is a systemic speculative activity in the financial institution industry.

As the trading volume for the Bank of America is high, it makes it a good liquid stock. Similarly, JP Morgan and Citigroup also make popular trading stocks. All of them exhibit some top trading volumes, which are visible signals for day traders to enter a position and exit in a short window of time.

Social Media Stocks

This industry is being considered as a lucrative target by day traders. Facebook and Twitter, the two giants of the social media industry, exhibit some high volumes of trading in their stocks. There have been unending debates over the power of these giants to transform their user-base into a revenue stream that is big as well as well-sustained. As the number of social media users grows across the world with the expansion in the broadband internet across different continents, the social media industry is the hotspot for advertisers and big business, which makes sure that the industry is consistently injected with big cash. As a result, trading volume in the stocks of the social media industry remains high, making the industry popular among day traders (Hall, 2019). Still, which stocks you have to buy depends on a wide range of factors including your experience. The tips I have discussed in this chapter are for the absolute beginners in the world of day trading.

You need to determine which level of risk you can afford during your investing ventures. You ought to focus on creating a strategy for picking stocks to keep your capital intact so that you can stay in the game. If you succeed in preserving the capital, you will most likely start making money in the long run. Each stock has a different level of volatility, volume, and price features. You need to start with lower risk portfolios and then keep moving to minimize the risk. As you make more moves, you will learn how to make informed and educated decisions.

Chapter 5: Psychology and Mindset of a Successful Day Trader

Trading in financial markets can be a bumpy road if you feel that your mental energy is no more and that you cannot focus on the markets anymore. Luckily, you can resolve this problem and start enjoying trading once again by improving your mindset. Some people opine that stock markets are generally immoral but the fact is that stock markets are neither immoral nor moral. Stock markets lack emotions that's why it is up to you how you perceive the stock market to behave. If you want to enter the business of the stock market for the long term and also establish yourself as a full-time day trader, you must develop a specific mindset that aids you in observing the stock market from an unemotional point of view.

It is your mindset that will control your reactions to different transactions. It is your mindset that will help you define how you react to lost trades and big profits. Your mindset will define how you can stay calm during turbulent times and how you can avoid reacting based on emotions. A trader who is disciplined and who has a strong mindset will never let emotions meddle with his or her decisions regarding the stock market. If this sounds hard for you, don't worry because it should sound hard for every beginner. It takes a bit of effort to achieve that status. There is no way by which you can become a successful trader overnight. Trading is just like another business. As you cannot become a successful businessman overnight, you cannot become a disciplined trader overnight. You need to give yourself time to achieve the success that you are looking forward to.

Importance of a Positive Mindset

The stock market is void of emotions but the participants of the markets are usually full of them. This is the reason reading chart patterns and trends work so well when it comes to trading. They show us some well-known patterns that humans possess. That's how as a trader you can take advantage of the market psychology. There is a notorious saying that 90% of traders lose 90% of funds in 90 days. This is wicked, to say the least, but still, this phrase is popular among traders. Before you take the leap in the stock market, you should ask yourself what are the psychological traits that 10% of the remaining traders have. What qualities they possess that make them different from the rest of the lot. If 90% fails, the money they have lost has surely gone to the 10% who succeeded. That's intriguing! Isn't it? When you lose, someone is earning on your money. The people who are earning on your money are humans just like you. They are a small bunch of traders who have found the secret of trading, which is nothing else but a trader's mindset. The term trading psychology refers to a specific state of mind that a trader usually has while he or she trades. If you don't have the right mindset, the odds will likely be turned against you.

Shape up Your Trader's Mindset

Traders can reshape their mindset by acting in a calm and relaxed manner. If you have proper knowledge of the subject and you have kept in place proper risk management guidelines, you need not be concerned about your trades at all. If a trade hits the stop-loss level, it doesn't mean that the world has ended for you. Traders lose trades all the time. It happens to even professional traders who have years of experience. Professional traders whose bread and butter rely on trading stocks have a winning rate of 50%. Even at this rate, you can bag sufficient profits on your capital if you trade with the right mindset.

You should practice the habit of not taking a losing trade to heart. There is nothing personal in a lost trade although the temptation to make it personal runs high. The thought may start spinning in your head that you have lost something you could have easily won or you could have easily prevented. If you think like that, the need of the hour is to train your brain into thinking that markets tend to go upside and downside almost all the time. As a day trader, you should keep faith in the market analysis that you have already done. Just stick to the plan until the end of the day. Markets are void of emotions and if you start succumbing to your emotions, you will not be able to compete with the traders who don't let their emotions meddle in their trading transactions over the day. Try to nurture a morning routine for a more relaxed trading session. Try to wake up earlier, do some workout or a yoga session, and then sit on your desk with a heart full of faith in the homework you have done for the day.

Learn! Learn! Learn!

The education of the stock market is the key to success. It is one of the most important factors that play a key role in removing fear from your brain. This is what separates an average trader from a successful trader. Even if you have nurtured and developed the right mindset for trading, you cannot succeed until you have a solid knowledge base for the purpose. You must have a solid understanding of the reasons behind the price movements and market reactions. For example, I have discussed in the past chapters about how the price of a stock moves upward or downward when the volume goes through a particular change. Similarly, I have hinted on how a market reacts to certain news and regular bonus reports. This will add more strength to your trader mindset. There are lots of concepts that are worth learning. However, you cannot learn them in a single session. You should make it a habit to internalize a concept daily so that your brain gets enough time to understand the slight nuances in the concept and to use the same during trading without having to open a book. You also can prepare and keep notes in a small diary for reference. You can form a healthy routine by consuming an hour before going to bed a good book on trading to clear out your basic concepts and bring them into practice during trading. You also can enroll in trading courses to boost your knowledge about stock markets.

The Mindset of a Successful Trader

Your psychology is going to be the major determining factor in bringing about the trading results that you are aiming at. Each trader keeps a unique belief system and it is their beliefs that determine how they trade and what results they get. The traders that have a weak belief system tend to fail even if they have the most profitable and seasoned trading strategy. What is a belief system? In simple words, it is called 'The Trader's Mindset.'

When you go through psychological issues, it is in your best interest to track the issues in your brain, recognize them, and then find a cure for them. Otherwise, you cannot fix them. A psychologist recognizes the issues and then tries to cure the patient. The process of curing a problem can take longer because the patients take long to recognize the problem and accept it as the source of their downfall. As a day trader, you need to take responsibility for your problems if you want to heal yourself. Success in trading is directly proportional to a sound and operational tracking system of your brain. It also is directly linked to a successful money management strategy, sound psychology, and proper capitalization during the day. These need to be in proper sync if you want to be successful in your trading ventures. Mastering your psychology is very well an ongoing process that goes on end until you are in control of your thoughts and decisions.

Psychological Issues

The biggest psychological issue that day traders may confront is the fear of being stopped out or the fear of posting a loss and exiting a position. It is almost a nightmare for day traders, and it definitely weakens their nerves. The basic reason behind this behavior is that a trader is afraid of failure, and he feels as if he will not be able to bear the loss. His ego is well at stake. If you are getting out of a trade too early, you are losing profit if not capital. It becomes quite common for a trader to exit a position to relieve himself of anxiety and stress that an open position usually brings. The biggest fear in this sense is the fear of reversal. Traders succumb to it once it grows to an unprecedented level. They need gratification and a sense of security that their capital is safe now.

The biggest mistake that day traders make is adding on to the position they are losing. They just keep doubling down on it. This kind of act alludes to a mindset that doesn't want to accept that it has lost the game. Here again, ego won't let you close your position and save your capital. Your brain presses on winning out of the same position in which you have lost. The problem gets more intense if you have disclosed your positions to your colleagues and family members. You fear to become a laughing stock in front of everyone.

Some traders don't want to take responsibility for their trades. They cannot accept the fact that the market went in the opposite direction than they had accepted it to move. This kind of mindset fogs their brain and they try to create a reality that is aligned with their expectations. Sometimes traders enter the gambler's mindset. They fall prey to the euphoria of a bull market and get drowned in it by slipping into gambling. The gambler mindset always tells you to ignore the indicators of the market and compels you to indulge in compulsive trading even when the odds are against it. Trading becomes your addiction. You keep losing until your capital is wiped out. This is very dangerous and it needs a check.

Some people start getting angry after they lose a trading position. Their brain tells them that they are victims of the trade market. There are unrealistic expectations that when the shattered result in frustration and anger among traders. This condition can strike you if you are getting too much involved in a trade. You cannot control the market and turn it in your favor just by thinking that way. You might have expected the stock to rise during the day but markets can take an ugly turn anytime, leaving you flabbergasted. Too many expectations can lead to anger that can affect your future trading transactions. Not good for your profession. Just as excessive anger is bad for the health of your brain, excessive joy after you win a trading position is also bad. This indicates a mindset that makes you feel that you are unrealistically in control of the trade markets.

A typical kind of mindset may compel you not to follow a certain trading system. Some traders don't believe in the existence of a certain trading system. They think that the markets don't follow a certain course. They move spontaneously without following any indicators. This mindset indicates weakness and an unwillingness to do the due amount of homework. After all, it takes time, energy and an iron will to sift through books, papers, and scan charts, and graphs and figures. Some people are willing to work on the research material but they are deluded into believing that stock markets just don't follow a set trading system. Some people think that becoming a nerd doesn't suit their personality. This kind of mindset is bad for trading for the long term. There is no way by which you can trust your ability over a successful trading system.

Another common mindset is overthinking about your trade and keep second-guessing the trade signals. For example, the volume has indicated that you must buy or sell and you keep waiting for a second indicator to make your move. If your brain asks you to find out a sure thing then I must disappoint you that sure things just don't exist in the stock market business. Sometimes, it happens that you start thinking about the outcome of a transaction before making the move. The outcome is always unknown and you cannot simply predict it at all. If your brain is not willing to accept the unknown, it is not a trader's brain. Some traders complain that they start feeling irritated after the trading day. They are overwhelmed by an emotional rollercoaster of fear, anger, and greed. This happens because they put too much emphasis on the results of trading instead of the process and the skills of trading. Unrealistic expectations about your trading positions can make you feel irritated.

All the issues I mentioned above are psychological and are very common. They revolve around the fact that a trader doesn't follow the chosen trading strategy or the system. Instead of that, he prefers to trade his emotions which ultimately land them in trouble (Mcdowell, 2009).

Create Discipline

Discipline is the key to success in day trading. The market is there to offer you a thick bundle of opportunities regarding trade. You get the opportunity to trade thousands of products and different currencies every second of the day yet not all seconds are destined to go in your favor. There are just a few of them which can benefit you during the day. There is usually a five-second window that you need to exploit your trading opportunities. It doesn't mean that a single trade lasts for five seconds and it ends, but it means that a single trade spans over just five seconds of activity. Usually, one second is spent on placing an order. Then you have to wait before you start an activity again. A few seconds are spent on placing stops and targets on the order. This is how you complete the five seconds window. The main point is that the actual trading time spans over a fraction of the day even if you consider yourself an active trader. The rest of the time you have to spend is on sitting, watching, and waiting. That's where you need lots of discipline. Unless you wait for the right trade signals, you cannot take benefit from them. When you see one, you must make haste without any hesitation so that the opportunity is not lost. This demands that you remain actively present in front of the trading screens.

Trading demands great discipline when there is hardly any opportunities present. You need to stay alert for opportunities. The discipline is also mandatory for acting instantaneously whenever you see any opportunity. Once a trader has entered a position, he needs the discipline to follow the trading strategy he has made earlier on. You budge from the trading strategy, you drown yourself in the pool of losses.

Patience

Patience is also related to discipline. Trading demands patience as you have to wait for a considerable length of time after you place an order. Sometimes, the wait starts from the morning and ends just before the trading closes in the evening. Many traders can enter or exit the market at inopportune times, saying that their timing was off. When they run out of patience, they start jumping in or out of trades without a plan. Sometimes, they do that too soon and sometimes they do that too late, which lands them in grave trouble. Seasoned traders learn to wait over time but new traders lose patience so soon. Trading demands that you wait with patience for the perfect entry and exit opportunities in the market. Wait until you see a trade signal and then act swiftly to grab the moment. It is highly likely that you have waited for three hours and then you have to act in three seconds to take benefit of your trading position. This is how you have to balance your trade with patience and action. If you can do this, you can make money and also make a name in the world of day trading.

Ways to Acquire a Trader Mindset

The statistics are not quite positive for day traders as 80% of them are likely to lose money at one point or another. Usually, there is plenty of pressure on them for making money when you adopt da trading as a full-time job. You pile up the pressure because you have to run your household with the money you earn from day trading. When you cannot do that and miss a day, you get under pressure that keeps mounting until you succeed in earning some money. But throughout the time you fail to earn, you are losing some. So, if you have lost $5,000 of your capital and have earned $2,500 back, you have failed. You have lost the entire $5,000 because the $2,500 you have earned back is likely to be spent on your daily expenditures. However, if you have a day job by which you can add up to your trading account quickly, you will face less pressure. Once the pressure of making money for daily expenditures is lifted from your nerves, you will be less inclined toward making emotional decisions. You will be able to maintain patience. There will be no quick profit-making or insane loss cutting. This is how you can be able to keep your head in the right condition.

Some traders get proper education on how to formulate a brilliant trading strategy and how to implement it, but they lose their calm along the way, which results in their losses. Day traders use a term called loss aversion, which means that losses can have a deep psychological impact on the brains of day traders. The impact is far greater than the positive effect that making gains in the stock market has. When a person loses $1,000 he or she feels more pain then making $1,000 in profits. The scale of pain is way higher. This kind of mindset can make a trader hold on to losing trades for a longer period. They expect that they can earn their lost capital from the same stock once again.

You can avoid this kind of fallout in your brain by defining how much capital you can put on stake. Losses are bound to happen in the stock market because stock markets have a bad habit of proving even seasoned traders wrong by taking awkward turns. Avoiding losses means that you don't have to let your ego get in your way when you are losing a trade. A healthy trader mindset is the one that tells you to let go of the trade. These are false hopes that the trade that has inflicted so much loss and pain on you will bring about profits for you. It can do that for some other day but over the same day, such expectations are the choice of the unwise.

Keep in check the emotions of greed when you are day trading. There comes a time when you are making lots of profit from trade. You can do that once or twice but you must not stick to it to make more. Once a stock has exhausted its run in the market, it can reverse any time and you will be left empty-handed, losing all the gains to the brutal reversal of the stock. The best strategy is to trace the signals and technical indicators and then stick to your strategy. When your calculations tell you to move out of your position, do that. Otherwise, you will see your trades turning against you, stripping you of early gains. This can be frustrating.

As a day trader, you need a plan for your day trading such as which stock to choose and how to choose it as I have discussed in the past chapters. Once you have made a plan and chosen stock for trading, a trader mindset demands that you stick to the plan by exhibiting strict discipline. If you can do that, you will be able to kill emotional trading. You will have the satisfaction that you have a strategy that you must follow to stay in control of your trading positions. This will help you prevent shooting out of your trades over fears of reversal in trades.

How to Achieve Emotional Stability

Emotional stability is the key to becoming a successful trader. It is unsatisfactory to see how little control people possess over their brains and their attention. You know a little about the processes that tend to shape your behavior in the world. The common weakness among human beings is that they cannot sit quietly in a place. They need some activity all the time which engages their brain and body. If you learn to sit quietly for considerable lengths of time, the activity can teach you to see the stock markets as they are, to bear the pain, and to walk without a hint of regret. You need to sit, relax, and be quiet. You can do that on a cushion, on a bench, on a chair, or under a tree in some outdoor location. You can sit anytime in the morning, during the night and in the afternoon. Loosen up your waist to let your stomach sit freely as you breathe more air in and out. You need to sit with a straight back and an upright head. Try to find a focal point such as breathing. It is a good place to start. Breathe naturally through your nose. When you start getting distracted by sights, sounds, thoughts, and emotions, bring back your focus to breathing. Try to keep track of your breath as it goes in and comes out. You can do it for 20 minutes during the day and more if you can just sit quietly and keep your attention intact. If you practice it each, it will help you maintain emotional stability, which is the key to success in the stock market.

Laughing has magical powers when it comes to healing your brain and body. Some people even claim that laughing can cure cancer over time. When you are having a good laugh, you are fine-tuning your brain to downplay the effect of any tragedy you have been through. Laughter can put you in a positive mindset and help you wear off the effect of a bad trade that just happened. Earlier on, I have talked about how a trader can stay irritated even on the next day of a bad trade. Healthy laughter can help you minimize the adverse effect of bad trading on your brain, making you more stable.

Emotional stability revolves around the conditioning of the brain. As a day trader, you are bound to witness some really bad situations when you see your hard-earned money melt into thin air. These are the times when you can remember a positive memory from the past and use it to smile. Tell your brain that tough times are destined to pass. Dark times herald good times. You can search for some old photos that can make you smile. When you smile and think positively, it becomes easier to face the challenges and also make healthy and wise decisions to tackle problems. The stock market is like life itself. It is full of problems with a few silver linings.

Exercise releases endorphins that act as a powerful pill. Everyone feels really good after a powerful session of exercise. An exercise can be a walk down the road or on the beach. Just keep your mind empty while you exercise and try to give room to new exciting ideas. You also can try to find out answers to the questions that are stuck in your brain. You can go to the gym for an intense workout session or you can play tennis with a friend. Exercise helps you deal with intense pressure which can help deal with the pressure that emanates from intense day trading sessions.

You can do meditation as well to help you battle out the bad times of your life. Tough times have a problem that they tend to last for a while. Your brain allows them to linger on for a longer period than they should have. Meditation can rewire your brain and help you drive out the thoughts that have been stuck for quite some time. You can enroll in an online meditation program or you can go to attend a physical session. You also can buy a guided meditation book to follow step by step instructions through headphones. Meditation will help you enjoy the real calmness of mind. It will correct your breathing and allow you to get relaxed. After each meditation session, you will find yourself in a better mindset.

So, emotional stability is the key to success in day trading. Just imagine what good is in there if you find yourself in frenzy each time you post a loss. You will ruin your future trades as well, which is something that you will not want to happen. The biggest mistake day traders make is to keep everything to themselves. If you have a reliable and sensible spouse, let it out in front of him or her. If you have a friend, tell him or her what you went through. Reveal to them how bad the day was or how good the day was. Write in a diary about your experiences during the past day. When you reveal everything from the past day, it becomes your catharsis, which in turn resets your emotions and cures them. You also can say it out loud in your bedroom. By doing these activities, you help yourself deal with your trading problems effectively. It will also stabilize your thoughts. Our brain acts like a pressure cooker. When there is an excess of activity in the brain and a frequent spinning of thoughts, it starts acting awkwardly. Your behavior changes, your language changes and you act like a disturbed person. Therefore, if you let it all out, you regain calmness, and your emotions stabilize.

Last but not least thing is to nurture a dream in your heart. Everyone who wants to succeed in life needs a dream to follow up. A dream of a bright future always exists in the hearts of a majority of people. People dream of a life they want to enjoy. The dream can be of a great mansion you might have come across while on your way to the countryside. It can be of a supercar that you might have seen cruising on the road. The dream can be of an ultra-fast cruise ship that you might want to take for a ride across the Mediterranean Sea. It is easy and almost necessary to dream when you are young. Dreaming big is something that can bring about emotional calm and stability for you because each time you start losing cool, you think about the dreams you have yet to achieve.

At times, reality can hit you and it becomes highly tempting to give up on your dreams. Your brain tries to bring your dreams closer to reality to achieve a sense of gratification and satisfaction. For example, a close-to-reality dream can be something easy to get. However, if you study the lives of extraordinary people who truly succeeded, you will know that they never let that temptation affect their brains. They never stopped dreaming, believing in their abilities and moving forward to the destination they once had imagined. You can get a trader mindset if you never stop believing in your dreams.

When you have decided to pursue your dreams, you automatically get in the mindset of developing good habits such as completing 6-8 hours of sound sleep, going to bed early in the night, and getting to bed early in the morning. A full night of good sleep is the best medicine to handle troubles and move forward in the right direction. Your dreams compel you to drive out the bad habits and welcome good habits. When you know your direction, you wield more control over your body and brain. It will boost your confidence when you start day trading.

Chapter 6: An Overview of Proven Day Trading Strategies

A day trading strategy circles around a set of trading rules to follow so you can successfully enter and exit a trading position during the day. Many trading strategies are built on different indicators and signals that you can use. Multiple indicators tend to give different results. The foremost thing is that your trading strategy needs to involve a bunch of clear rules for when to open and when to close a trade. The more you base them on technical criteria, the easier it is for you to implement them. There is usually no space for personal thoughts. There should be minimum hesitation in the decision-making process as well.

A good trading strategy needs to involve a bunch of effective stop-loss rules. It limits the risk involved in the transaction. It is good to limit the risk to 1-2% of the bankroll in a transaction. In this way, you will need 50-100 consecutive losing trade to wash your hands off all funds in the account. If you decide to follow a trading strategy, you make sure that you are not losing your capital in the blink of an eye. A good trading strategy should have a success rate which is higher than the losses. A 50 % success rate means that 5 out of 10 trades are successful which is acceptable for a trader who is just starting. You should have a risk-to-return ratio of 1 to 10. It means that when you are risking one, you are aiming at getting 10. However, it is only possible when you have plenty of experience in this field.

High-frequency Trading (HFT)

High-frequency trading is usually conducted with the help of powerful computers that operate on complex algorithms for analyzing stock markets. They buy and sell shares in a matter of seconds. They operate on specialized software. You will have to buy a high-end computer to successfully do HFT. HFT offers you benefit which regular traders lack in general. This kind of trading existed before crypto currency and is now estimated to make up a whopping 80% of the total volume in different asset markets. It is now becoming a decisive factor in the realm of decentralized assets, and more investors are starting to take notice of this trading strategy.

The basic principle behind HFT strategies demands that the ones who are executing them are the first to execute that as it takes a fraction of a second to make a profitable move an unprofitable one. There are a bunch of techniques that traders can use to stay afloat in a neck-on-neck competition. Top investment banks, hedge funds, and financial institutions usually carry out HFT. They employ experts who use automated trading platforms for making profits. However, now high-frequency trading firms have come into place to do the job.

HFT, as already mentioned, runs on a set of complex algorithms that study the market, learns from it, and make decisions in a split second. These algorithms can spot the latest emerging and developing trends in the markets across the globe and kick off trading on them before human players get a chance to trade and bag profits on the same. These superfast computers place huge volumes of trades across multiple markets to double up profits on the trade transactions they make over time. If you compare their trade transactions and profits with the ones carried out by human players, you will see the visible difference in the giant size of the profit that HFT brings for you. They have the power to convert small margins into big margins. These systems do achieve this otherwise tough feat by their enormous speed of making money. They generally capitalize on the theory that high-end tech can raise the level of profits from the stock markets. However, high-speed trading companies don't enjoy a good reputation as compared to manual trading. More often they are viewed as rogue players that are aiming at getting an edge over their competitors at all costs.

The techniques involved in this kind of method are arbitrage, colocation, pinging, market-making, and news-based trading. Each option has its costs and benefits. Colocation is the practice of installing a trading server as close to the data center of the exchange as it is possible to avoid the delays in data transmission from the markets. The fastest the system is fed with market data, the quicker it will act to make profits. On regular exchanges, every trader is at risk of losing capital because of delays in the transmission of data. Retail investors are used to this kind of delays but HFT systems can make or lose money in milliseconds. The best strategy is to buy the best tech equipment that is available in the market and the other, as I just told you, transporting your server as close to the data center as you can. Some traders set up shops in the area close to the data center. These exchanges often house private servers for the interested traders. You also can have a cross-connection that links to the main server of the data center, which helps you circumvent connecting through the internet. This ultimately cuts the undue delays and this translates into catching up with some big profits.

An HFT strategy is a market-making strategy in the trading world. It can be spotted whenever a trader who has adequate resources in hand places bids and asks in the stock market. This act of his offers liquidity and gives him profit that is based upon spread. Market-making is generally provided by big firms and it is considered as a positive practice to keep important markets liquid. HFT market makers are firms that don't have any contracts with the exchange. They leverage their top speed and improved performance to make sure that it is their bids and asks that drive and shape the markets.

Another HFT strategy is arbitrage which is the act of taking advantage of the difference in the price of the same stock on multiple markets. It happens that a single stock has inconsistent prices across different exchanges. Traders often locate the difference and exploit it to make profits. In crypto currency, the frequency of arbitrage is higher than the ordinary markets therefore it offers a greater opportunity for making profits. Regular traders can reap benefits of these abnormalities in the market but here again, HFT traders, are at a greater advantage of these situations. They can use software that is designed to detect discrepancies fast. In the same fast manner, they can create orders in response. They are capable of detecting the variations in prices of the same asset and jumping on to make your move faster than others. As it is related to speed, HFT traders leverage their ability to work fast and efficiently (Edwood, 2020).

The method, however, just like others, has its flaws. First of all, it is considered a controversial method of trading that tends to strip you of human decision-making. Trades usually take place in a split second which can create flash lows and highs in the stock market without any reason or warning. It means that a single bad order or a glitch in the algorithm or computer system can result in the loss of millions of pounds in a matter of seconds. This kind of market volatility can result in a ripple effect in the stock market. There have been concerns by the Financial Conduct Authority that it can put small investors at a greater disadvantage and can eventually distort the shape of markets. There is another risk that watchdogs cannot detect potential wrongdoing.

Penny Stocks

Day trading in penny stocks is gaining steam due to a lower barrier of entry and the ability to earn a big amount of money. Savvy investors who learn the art of making money with penny stocks can bag big profits. Still, we cannot deny the fact that a vast majority of people tend to lose their capital in a matter of days just because they don't follow the right strategy. Trading in penny stocks is different from trading in the normal stock market therefore you need to make out the complications that are involved in this type of trading before you make a dive.

Penny stocks have different names such as small caps, micro caps, and stocks under $5. The most common aspect of penny stocks is that they are usually not listed on some big stock markets. Also, they demand a different approach from day traders. Normal stocks are generally listed on NASDAQ, New York Stock Exchange, Dow Jones, and other major stock markets. On the other hand, penny stocks are traded on Over the Counter markets. Most online brokers support these markets. You cannot label a stock that is listed on a traditional exchange as penny stock no matter how low its price is. If the shares of a major company sink to the bottom of the market, they don't become penny stocks. The downfall of a share comes due to a wide range of factors such as the bad reputation of the company and any negative news about the company.

Trading in penny stocks is very risky, to say the least. Most penny stock companies are highly volatile which puts regular traders in a risky position to lose their capital big times. However, risks are a part of the stock market game. You can still make big bucks by trading in penny stocks if you keep it smart and targeted. You need to know what you have to look for in the stock market. There are a bunch of characteristics by which you can tell if a penny stock will help you make money or not.

First of all, you must know that a company is on her way to making money. The company should be in good monetary health with positive reports flowing in for the near past. A company that is losing capital is not a good investment and this is true for the general stock market as well. It doesn't matter how low the share price is. What matters is the fact that the company is posting sufficient profits for the past few quarters. The second most important factor that you must keep into consideration is that the company you are investing in has sufficient cash to fulfill contingencies. Powerful companies need not liquidate their future viability to service debts. You must conduct in-depth research into whether the company has got enough cash for the purpose or not. Only invest in, if the answer is affirmative. What most investors ignore is the fact that penny stock companies don't like to remain penny stock companies. They are looking forward to grabbing the earliest opportunity to jump into the mainstream stock markets. Therefore, you need to scan the companies to find out a viable strategy to materialize their plan of jumping into mainstream markets. If a company has got a plan, it means it is aiming at gaining exponential growth to change its fate. This kind of company can help you make big money. The most common indicators of these plans include rebuilding a powerful and long-term business plan and paying back to investors.

When you have scanned a company for all the three pre-requisites and you are convinced about them, dive in to earn the money you are looking for. But wait! There is another problem in your way of making money. You cannot just scan all the penny stock companies. Just like we learned about choosing the best stock to trade, there should be a method to choose the best penny stock to invest in. On the penny stocks, the same rule applies: you need to pick one at a lower position and sell it when it rises. That's a challenge. How can you find a stock that is undervalued and is likely to break free and rise in price? You need to find a stock that is low in value and also has a positive outlook. Here is a pack of some proven strategies to trade in penny stock.

Find a day trader who is willing to sell the share at the bargain price. If the company is expecting a turnaround, the trader will hold on to the stock to enjoy the benefits, which makes the shares difficult to buy. Once you have purchased a lucrative penny stock, you need to make sure that you will be able to sell it. Hold on to it and wait for the right opportunity. When the time finally comes, sell it. You must realize that you have bought the shares at a lower price because it is undesirable at the moment. Its price is low because people are selling it. Therefore, it needs time to regain investors' confidence. This is the time you need to sell it without any further delay.

Penny stocks are not stable companies. They might be new companies who are looking for an island in the vast ocean of business to gasp for a while. They might be companies that are in grave danger of running out of business. Therefore, you need the right mindset to trade in penny stocks. When you are evaluating penny stocks, you need to take a look at some key indicators to analyze if a stock is likely to perform well shortly or not. There is usually no fundamental information available for penny stocks because they don't file necessary paperwork which is mandatory for large-cap stocks. You need to look around for a few positive and negative indicators based on which you can determine which penny stock is the best for investment.

The positive indicators for a penny stock are positive earnings by the company or presence of some fresh contracts that the company has signed. Fresh contracts indicate growth in business. Positive financing is another big indicator that you must keep knowledge of. Apart from those new partnerships sealed by the company indicate that company management is serious about growing its business. Just as with the large-cap stocks, penny stocks move on the back of some big volumes. If you see a rise in the volume of a stock, it is time to enter a position. At the last on the list of indicators is positive news about the particular industry.

The negative indicators include rumors that originate from the inside of the company. For example, employees of the company are saying badly about the future course of the company. A drop in the trading volume is a bad sign. Similarly, negative news about the particular industry indicates that the stock price is likely to drop in the short run. Therefore, you need to stay away from that.

You can buy penny stocks on some major exchanges as well but they are mostly traded on OTC exchanges. There are various reasons as to why they cannot be traded in big markets. A few of them are the size and profits of the company. There are usually thousands of penny stocks to choose from. The question is how you narrow down on the choices? You can use a stock screener for the purpose which allows you to filter the stocks based on a set criteria.

You also can create a strategy to win by trading in penny stocks. The first method is to educate yourself about the complications in OTC markets. The more knowledge you have about how penny stocks behave during the day, the better you will get to trade in them. Some traders make a grave mistake of getting complacent with the patterns of the stock market. The stock market constantly evolves through the day, the week, and the month. You cannot expect a method that has worked for you today to work for you tomorrow. Even if the indicators appear to be the same, you need to give a second look to the stock market to see if there is any slight change in volume or the news about a stock. You can always miss the news that can change the game while you are left wondering what just happened. You cannot blame the market if you are not adaptable to the changes that keep popping up throughout the day, the week of the year. Try to change your strategy over time.

A robust penny stock watch list is a must if you want to succeed in that business. If you want to stay on top of the opportunities, prepare this list. A watch list contains the stocks you want to invest in. The objective of creating this list is to monitor the penny stocks regularly to stay up to date. When their prices drop to what you had expected, pounce on them to grab them, and make a profit (Sykes, 2020).

Momentum Trading

Momentum trading is a technique in which traders make transactions according to the robustness of the recent trends in the price of a certain stock. Momentum in trading or price is similar to the momentum that you might have read in 5th-grade physics. In the momentum of physics, mass is multiplied by the velocity to determine the possibility of the object continues to go on the same path. In stock markets, momentum is calculated by different factors such as trading volume and the rate of the change in price. Momentum traders bet that the price of an asset is moving toward the upward trajectory is likely to move on the same path until the trend exhausts itself. This practice of trading started centuries ago. It can date back to the 1700s when a renowned British investor David Ricardo used momentum-based strategies to trade in the market. He used to buy stocks that were powerfully performing on the market and sold those that performed poorly. He focused on cutting short on the losses and capitalizing on the profits.

A relative momentum strategy is an offshoot of momentum trading. It is the practice of comparing the performance of an asset with the other one. Investors favor buying strong securities and sell the weaker ones. Absolute momentum strategy alludes to the behavior when the price of a particular security is compared with its previous performance.

To employ this strategy, you need to learn how to determine the momentum of a price over certain weeks or months. The first step is to determine the direction of the trend in which you want to trade. They may seek to establish an entry point for buying and selling the asset they are trading.

Just like with any other trading strategy, you need to find out the right momentum indicators. The factor on which momentum depends is volume. It is the amount of a particular asset traded inside of a given time frame. Volume, you know, means the number of assets traded in a particular time frame. Volume is crucial for momentum traders because they must be able to enter or exit certain positions faster. If a market has a higher number of buyers and sellers, it is labeled as a liquid market and is easier to trade in an asset for cash. Otherwise, it is dubbed as illiquid. Volatility is another factor that comes into consideration when we talk about momentum trading. It is the amount of change in the price of a certain asset. High volatility alludes to big price swings while low volatility alludes to stability in the price of an asset. Momentum traders seek out for volatile markets and assets to leverage on slight rises and fall in the price of an asset.

As a day trader, you have to look out for the asset you want to invest in. A momentum trader is generally concerned about the price action of a certain asset. This is why momentum traders need to rely heavily on technical analysis as well as indicators to determine their course of action. Here is the rundown of popular momentum indicators.

• Momentum Indicator is the most popular indicator available. It harvests the closing prices of assets and compares them to the previous closing prices, which can be used to analyze the trends in the markets. It is an oscillator and works as a single line that moves up and down on a chart. The value of the indicator line offers traders an idea of how fast the price is moving. If the reading is somewhere around 35, it indicates a faster uptrend as compared to reading around 30. If the reading is -20, it is a faster uptrend than -10. Some traders use the indicator to device their entry and exit plan but most traders use it for confirmation of the price action of an asset. If the indicator line crosses the zero line, traders should understand that the asset is gaining momentum. Similarly, a drop below zero indicates that the price is losing upward momentum and is now ripe to slide down to the bottom.

• Relative Strength Index (RSI) is another indicator that provides traders with buy and sell signals. Just like the momentum indicator, this one also is plotted on a particular chart. There is an oscillator that moves between zero and 100. It offers overbought and oversold signals for an asset. A value above 70 is considered overbought while anything below 30 is labeled as oversold. When you are using this indicator, keep in mind that just because it gives oversold and overbought signals doesn't mean that the trend will reverse. It is better to use it in combination with other indicators.

- Moving Averages are used to detect emerging trends in stock markets. They are about using a formula that would filter out fluctuations to exhibit a prevailing price trend. They are not momentum indicators but they can help traders see if a market is range-bound or not. If you are using moving averages, you should be aware of the fact that they show a lagging indicator, which means that you will only get the signal after the price has moved. This means that you are going to need the support of other indicators to make a true assessment of the prices in the market. Only then you can be able to pinpoint the right entry and exit points.

Chapter 7: Step-By-Step to a Successful Trade

Usually, the US stocks have over 8,000 stocks on the list but a typical day trader has access to only a fraction of them because they just fail to build a fortune due to lack of an effective trade strategy. They enter the market based on rumors and exit it empty-handed as a result. More often they play at the cost of their precious capital. Winning can be hard in the stock market if you lack discipline as a trader. You need to identify the right stocks to create a winning situation for you. Despite the presence of the learning curve, the effort to detect the right stock is worthwhile. In this chapter, I will walk you through different steps that are involved in the completion of a successful trade.

Building a Watchlist

There is a visible difference between a watchlist and a portfolio. Before you head off to a start, you should know that a portfolio is a collection of the stocks you own at a given time while a watchlist displays the securities that you own and also the ones that you have selected even if you don't have any investment in them. Watchlists give you insights into the stocks that you will eventually want to add to your personalized portfolio.

You should create watchlists based on some current factors. You also need to use your previous watchlists if there are any. They would remind you of the searches that you have done in the past and would also help you fine-tune your future searches. Go through the list more often and also plan a personal schedule of how you will be able to comb through the list and see if the stock matches your criteria. In case of negative signals, delete the stock and save your time to focus on other stocks on your watchlist.

Start with the broader sets and then narrow down your stocks while you tailor them down as per your needs. If you know about your requirements, you can weed out the stocks that don't fulfill them. The key is to keep the list up to date. As the stock market reinvents itself each day each hour, you ought to reinvent your watchlist in the same way.

It is the best strategy to keep an eye on the stocks that seem to be popular. Keep an eye on the upward and downward trends in the popular stocks. When you keep an eye on the rise and fall of certain stocks, you will be able to trim and tune your watchlist. You will no longer be needing to enter the stocks of only the big companies. Instead, you can prepare your watchlist for small companies.

While you prepare a watchlist, you should keep an eye on the candlesticks, dojis, and charts. The fluctuation of prices is another element to watch for. You can build an effective watchlist by collecting liquidity components in the stocks, adding scanned stock listings that meet general technical criteria. Rescanning the watchlist to see which stock is ripe for investment and which should be discarded from the list after a while is also the key strategy to add to your skillset.

For example, you can say that if a stock's volume has been unattractive for the past few days, the stock should be off of your watchlist. Deletion is necessary to unburden a watchlist. The shorter it is, the more you will be able to keep it into consideration.

Introduction to Candlesticks

Candlestick charts came into use after 1850. The credit for the development and use of these candlestick charts goes to Homma who was a trader from a town named Sakata in Japan. It is believed that his original ideas were gradually modified as well as refined over several years of trading. To create and study a candlestick chart, you ought to have a data set that contains the open, low, high, and close values for a particular period that you want to display in the chart.

The hollow portion of a candlestick is labeled as the body of the candlestick. Some also call it the real body. The long thin lines in the candlestick that are above and below the candlestick are labeled as shadows. These are also referred to as tails or wicks. These are high and low ranges. The high is the top of the upper shadow while the low is the bottom of the lower shadow. If the stock is closing higher than the opening price, a hollow candlestick will be drawn with the bottom of its body showing the opening price, and the top showing the closing price. If it closes lower than the opening price, there will be a filled candlestick with the top of its body showing the opening price and the bottom showing the closing price.

As compared to bar charts, a majority of traders prefer candlestick charts because they are appealing and also easier to interpret. Each candlestick represents a price action. Hollow candlesticks with a greater close than the open allude to buying pressure while filled candlesticks with a greater open than the close allude to selling pressure.

In this picture, the two candlesticks with dots below them can be taken as examples of hollow and filled candlesticks.

Long vs. Short

The long body candlestick shows intensified buying or selling pressures on a stock or a currency. On the contrary, shorter candlesticks allude to little price changes. They also represent the consolidation of the price. Long hollow candlesticks that you can see in the chart show buying pressure. The longer it is, the higher the stock or currency will close above the opening price. This shows that the price moves fast from the opening level to close and that buyers had been aggressive. Long hollow candlesticks show that the stocks are likely to remain bullish. After an extended period of declines in the prices, the long hollow candlesticks mark a support level.

Long black candlesticks show powerful selling pressure. The longer it is, the further it will be below the opening price. This shows that the prices significantly dropped from the opening position and that the sellers had been aggressive. After a long period of advance in the prices of a stock or currency, a long black candlestick can herald a resistance level. After a long drop in prices, a long black candlestick indicates panic selling.

Marubozu

More powerful are the Marubozu brothers that usually are in white and black. Marubozu don't have upper and lower shadows. A white Marubozu is formed when the opening price is equal to the low price and the closing price equals the high price. This shows that buyers are in control of the price action right from the first trade to the last one. A black Marubozu is formed when the opening price stands equal to the high price and the closing price stands equal to the low price. This shows that sellers are in control of the price action right from the first trade to the last trade.

Long vs Short Shadows

The upper shadows of a candlestick show the highest point of a session while a lower shadow shows the lowest point of a session. Candlesticks that have shorter shadows shows that most of the trading action stayed confined near the open and close prices. Longer shadows indicate an extension in the opening and closing prices.

Candlesticks that have a longer upper shadow and shorter lower shadow allude to the fact that buyers were in domination and that they bid prices higher, but ultimately sellers pulled the prices down. This contrast and high and low close created a long upper shadow. On the contrary, candlesticks that have a longer lower shadow and a shorter upper shadow will indicate that sellers dominated in the session and that they drove the prices to the bottom. It also indicates that buyers resurfaced, later on, to bid higher prices at the end of a session.

Spinning Tops

Candlesticks that have a long upper shadow and an equally long lower shadow with a small body are labeled as spinning tops. Spinning tops indicate a state of indecision in the markets. The real body whether it is hollow or filled represents little movement in the price from open to close. The upper and lower shadows show that both bears and bulls had been active in the last session and that neither of them could gain an upper hand in the market. A spinning top shows a kind of standoff between buyers and sellers.

Doji

A doji represents a very important type of candlesticks. It offers plenty of information on their own as well as by forming patterns. Doji form when the opening and closing points of security virtually stand equal. In a Doji, the upper and lower shadow can vary in length and the resulting doji looks like a cross, a plus sign, or an inverted cross.

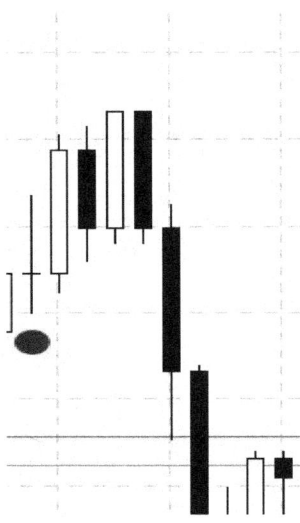

The open-close ought to be equal in an ideal state. This type of doji is considered robust. A doji indicates a tug of war between bulls and bears. Prices move up and down the opening level during a session. No one can gain control over the market. A doji that is formed among other candlesticks that have long bodies deemed more significant.

The relevance of a doji depends on its preceding candlesticks. After a long hollow candlestick, a doji indicates that buying pressure will weaken. After a fall in prices or a long black candlestick, a doji signals that selling pressure will start to diminish. Doji alone cannot mark an advance or reversal in the price.

After a long hollow candlestick, a doji points to a decreasing buying pressure. If there is a long black candlestick with a decline below the opening price after the doji, this alludes to bearish confirmation in the market. Therefore, after a long hollow candlestick, you should look out for an evening doji star.

If a doji comes after a long black candlestick, it shows selling pressure is diminishing and that the downward trend nears its end. A long hollow candlestick after that shows bullish confirmation so as a trader you should look out for this pattern which is commonly known as a potential morning doji star.

A long-legged doji has equal upper and lower halved. They represent indecision in the market. A long-legged doji indicates that the prices are trading above and below the opening level.

A dragonfly doji forms when the open, close, and high are equal, with the low creating a lower shadow. The candlestick will look like a T as there will be a shorter upper half. A dragonfly indicates that sellers are dominating the market and that the prices are dropping, but by the end of the session, the prices will circle back to the opening level.

Gravestone doji is formed when the opening, lower and closing prices are equal. The high will create a long upper shadow on the chart. The candlestick will look like an inverted T as there will be a short lower shadow. This indicates that buyers are dominating the market. However, by the end of the session, sellers will resurface and pull down the prices.

Miscellaneous Info

Long hollow candlesticks show that bulls are controlling the market. Long black candlesticks show that bears are controlling the market. Small candlesticks show that none of the two parties can move the ball and that the prices will circle back to where they started. A longer lower shadow alludes to bears who controlled the ball but bulls took over in the end. A long upper shadow indicates that bulls controlled the ball but bears took over in the end in a wild comeback. A long upper and lower shadow show that both bears and bulls had an equal chance in the game but neither could prove its mettle.

Hammer and Hanging Man

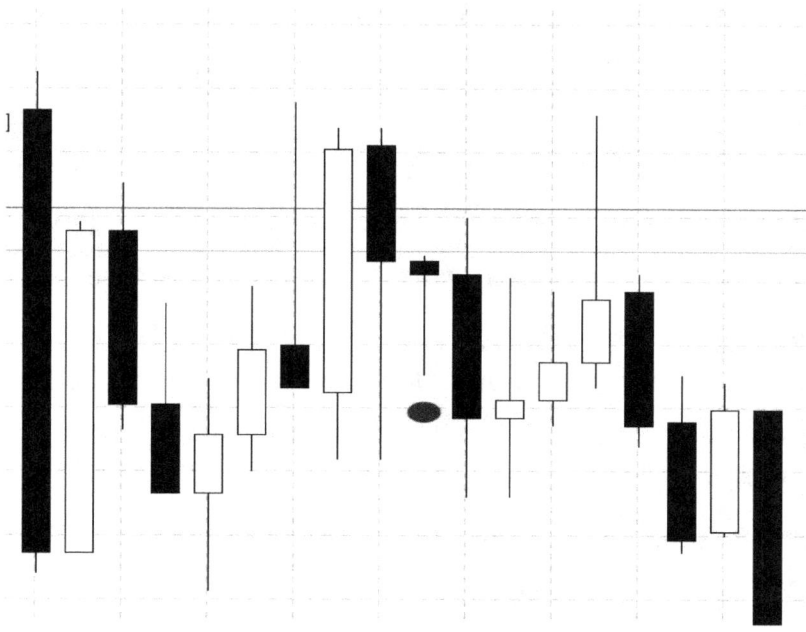

A hammer and hanging man look identical almost but they have different implications on the price action that just happened. As you see both have small bodies that can be black or white. Long lower shadows or non-existent upper shadows can also be seen in a hammer or hanging man. A hammer indicates a bullish reversal pattern that is usually formed when a reversal in price has already happened. The longer lowers shadow indicates that sellers ruled over the market session. This indication is sufficient to enter a buying position in the market. However, you should look out for further bullish confirmation. The lower part of the hammer is an indication that sellers remain in the market. If you see a long hollow candlestick after the hammer, this confirms further bullish trend. You are good to go now.

A hanging man indicates bearish reversal if it is succeeded by a long black candlestick on a big volume. Sell the position if you see this.

Exit Strategy

Financial markets are bound to take turns before they give you the desired profit you have been looking for. They usually move up and down based on different triggers such as news and different events. The traders who let the profits run out of greed or unawareness land themselves in trouble and incur hefty losses. It is vital to exit your trades at the right time to avoid imminent losses. If you establish well-tailored exit strategies, you can make your trades successful no matter what the circumstances in the market are. Sometimes a loss-averse trader misses out on an opportunity to avoid losses by not leaving the market when he could have got out of a position. Stop-loss orders are generally used to specify the price at which you should lose a position. When the price reaches this threshold, your broker will sell it by converting the position into a market order. This helps you cut down on the losses in case the price of the stock takes an unfortunate turn in a really fast manner. Another part of the exit strategy is to put a take-profit order. This will specify the price at which you can close a profitable position. Just like a stop-loss position, take-profit converts your order into a market order. There should be proper reasons behind these orders. You need to calculate the positions and make the decision accordingly as you will not want to close a profitable position that is likely to double up the profits in a matter of a couple of hours.

Support and Resistance

You can make use of the support and resistance levels that can help you in establishing your price targets. These are the points at which you should be willing to open or close a trading position. Support is the lower limit also known as the floor. There are a large number of traders who are willing to buy a stock at the support level. This causes an asset to bounce back after hitting the ground. Resistance is more or less the same. However, it resides at the upper level. It gathers sellers when the trading trend is going up. It makes the price to slide down to the opposite side. Trends tend to reverse at these specific levels that's why you can use price points to place stop-loss orders. You should set stop-loss orders just below the support and just above the resistance levels. This will help you give the stock price some room to fluctuate a little bit. You will not be thrown out of your position unceremoniously this way. You can use support and resistance to exit while using the take-profit option. You need to establish price targets to leave the trading position when you open a trading position. You need to do it with a risk-reward in mind. For example, if you risk $ 50 but you can earn $200 if the price reaches its target, the risk-reward is 1:3 (Common exit strategies in trading, 2018).

Moving Average Trailing Stops

Moving Average Trailing Stop is a money-management technique that tends to adjust either the existing stop or creates a new one. It uses the moving average indicator as a reference. Traders rely on it to decide where they should place their manual orders for positions. When you are using this strategy, stops are by default created and adjusted based on MA levels in real-time.

Moving averages tend to represent a highly popular way to set stop-loss points as you can calculate them easily and track them in the market in real-time. Some key moving averages include 5-, 9-, 50-, 200- day averages of a particular stock. You can apply them to a stock chart and determine whether the stock price reacted to these averages in the past or not as a resistance of support level.

Online brokers are always on the lookout for different strategies to put a limit on the losses of investors. One of the most common protection mechanisms is the stop-loss order of which I have given you a brief introduction in the past section. A trader can enhance their efficacy by pairing up the stop-loss strategy with the trailing stop. A trailing stop is a trade order where your stop-loss price stays unfixed as a single and absolute dollar amount. Instead, it is set at a specific percentage or a dollar amount just underneath the market price. When the price moves in the upward trajectory, it pulls the trailing stop with it. When it stops, the new stop-loss sets at the new level. That's how it protects the trader from losses while the profits soar to the sky-high. Trailing stops can be used with stocks, futures, and options.

If a stock soars to $10.97, the trailing stop will be $10.77. If its last price drops to $10.90, the stop value will be intact at $10.77. If the price further drops down to $10.76, it will penetrate the stop-level and kick off the market order. The order will be submitted at $10.76. Let's assume that the bid price was $10.75, the position will be closed at the same price. The net profit will be $0.75 per share. When the price slips for a while, you must resist an impulse to reset the trailing stop or your effective stop-loss will end up at a lower position than was expected. When you combine stop-losses with trailing stops, you should calculate the risk tolerance. There are many ways to trail the stop loss.

Volatility

Any kind of instrument that experiences a shift in the price tends to exhibit volatility of some scale. The change in the price can be positive or negative. Volatility trading refers to trading the volatility of some financial instruments instead of trading the price. Traders who tend to trade on volatility don't worry about which direction the price moves. They are simply trading the volatility and that's enough for them. Financial markets can be volatile at times with some big swings in price on a monthly or daily basis. In the absence of volatility, there usually is no profit potential in financial markets. Volatility is mostly associated with high risks but it is a fact that it can lead you to big returns on your money if you trade it correctly. Volatility is measured by using the standard deviation process, which calculates how far the current price of a stock trades relative to the moving average. Macro-economic data, news, political turbulence, national and international factors can have a significant impact on the level of volatility. Traders who trade volatility are usually not interested in the direction of price movements. They make profit on rising volatility no matter if the price shoots up or down. You can take big advantage of volatility with the help of a feasible trading strategy.

Straddle strategy is considered one of the highly popular strategies to take advantage of rising volatility in the price of a stock. The strategy returns profit when the price powerfully moves in one direction to the upside or the downside. This strategy is the best option if you use it during the periods when you are expecting high levels of volatility such as at a time before announcements of important market reports. When you use it with pending orders, you should identify a market that is in the consolidation phase before an important market release. Place a buy stop pending order in the market just above the top consolidation resistance. Also, place a sell stop pending order right underneath the lower consolidation support. Pending orders become market orders once pre-specified conditions can be met. For example, a buy stop order becomes a buy market order when the stock market hits a pre-specified price from the downside. A sell stop order converts into a sell market order once the market reaches a pre-specified price from the top. If the sell stop order is triggered for conversion, a stop-loss ought to be placed above the lower level of price consolidation, which ought to act as a resistance level once broken. Important market reports can shake the markets and create humongous volatility, especially, if they differ from the market expectations up to a greater extent (Konchar 2019).

Chapter 8: Understanding Trading Orders

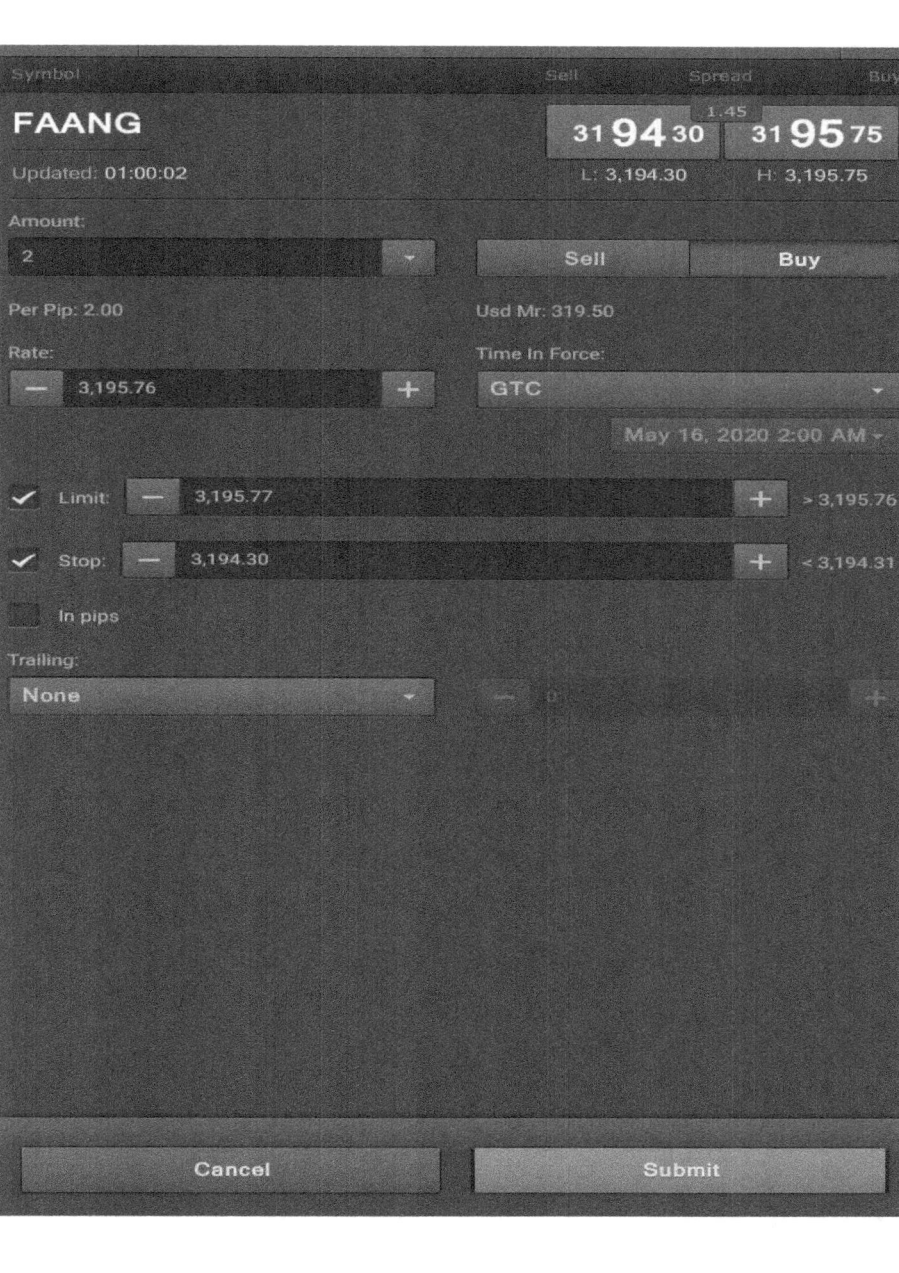

Trading mechanisms refer to the logistics that is behind trading securities and assets. This is regardless of the markets and trading types. The mechanism, for the most part, is the same. Different markets can be dealers, OTC, or big exchanges. The trading mechanism is the operation that traders have to go through. It is the mechanism that connects buyers with sellers and vice versa. This chapter will walk you through the ins and outs of the trading mechanisms, the types of markets, the techniques of placing an order, selling a position, and other related things.

To start with let's analyze the two basic types of trading mechanisms which are quote driven markets and order-driven markets. In a quote driven market, buyers and sellers provide quotes. As market makers provide these prices, these systems are suited to OTC makers or dealers. The other system is the order-driven system. Sellers and buyers grab control of the market. They place orders for certain assets that they desire to buy or sell. They list the assets at the market price and the market executes them instantly at the top available price.

Also, buyers and sellers can list the asset at a fixed price with a limit or stop order so that the order is not executed until the desired conditions are met with. Order mechanisms are well-suited to exchanges. Orders are immediately executed once a suitable counterparty is detected for a buyer and a seller. Simply put, a buy order will execute only if there is a seller in the market, who is willing to sell at the price range you have specified. The same is the case with the sell order.

Usually, sellers are listed in an ascending order and buy orders are listed in the descending order in the list of securities. These are sorted based on the list price. Order driven market works on a certain trading mechanism in which the lowest sell order ought to match the top buy order. Order books, that contain your orders, keep updating as you place new orders in the market.

There are a few disadvantages to the order-driven market. It will have a lower level of liquidity than the quote driven market. A market maker, in a quote driven market, is always willing to buy or sell as long as you are willing to take on the higher premiums of the quoted price. In order-driven markets, there is a possibility that trades can stagnate for a while if you don't find buyers who could buy at a certain price or vice versa. Order driven trading mechanisms, based on these automated matching systems, seem to be more suitable for the assets that are favorites of traders and that have a tendency to remain liquid. Order driven markets include bonds, stocks, options, and currencies. There are a lot of order types that a trader can take benefit of.

Market Order

A market order can be defined as a trade order for buying or selling a stock at the current price. You don't control the price at which you have to buy or sell a stock. It is the market that controls it. There is a higher level of slippage risk involved in the market order as the market sometimes moves fast. If a stock is being heavily traded in the market, there may be a lot of trade orders that need execution before you order. This can change the price of buying or selling. You may end up selling order at a much lower price than you might have thought or you may buy it at a much higher price than you had previously planned. So, with a market order, you have lesser control over the market.

Limit Order

The second on the list is the limit order which is a trade order for buying or selling a stock at a particular price or even better than that. A limit order tends to prevent traders from buying or selling at a price that they don't desire. If the market price does not seem to be in line with the order price, the order is unlikely to be executed. A limit order ought to be referred to as a sell limit order or a buy limit order.

A buy limit order is for buyers. It specifies that a buyer will not pay more than a certain price for a share of any company. It sets a buying price limit. For example, you should consider a stock with a price tag of $15. A trader tends to set a limit order for buying 100 shares for $14. The trade will only execute if the price of that stock comes down to $14 or lower than that.

Similarly, a sell limit order protects your investments from waste by selling too quickly at market price with plenty of risks. The seller, who has a sell limit order in place, will not sell the stock below a certain price. Only when the stock reaches or crosses the price bar, the trade will be executed. Take the example of the same stock that is valued at $15. You need to sell 100 shares at $17. The trade will only execute once the share price reaches $17. Otherwise, the order will remain on hold.

Stop-order

A stop order is referred to as a stop-loss order. It is a trade that is designed to limit and protect a trader from loss in a certain position. A stop order will sell a stock when it would reach a certain price. A stop order is generally associated with a long position but it can also be used with a shorter position. The stock is likely to be purchased if it is trading above the price of the stop order.

Take an example. A trader decides to sell a position. If it glides backward to $5 from its current position of $8, he or she would place a stop order at $5 so that when the price drops, the sale order is executed and he or she saves himself from a bigger loss.

One drawback is that the trader who could have sold it at $8, will have to sell it lower than that. Another problem is that the stock will not necessarily sell at $5. It depends on the supply and demand of the particular stock. If the stock is falling fast, the order is likely to be executed at a lower price than $5 as there should be lots of sale orders by thousands of traders.

Stock-limit Order

A stock-limit order is a trade order that tends to feature a stop and limit order. It requires the placement of two prices which is a stop and a limit price. Once a particular stock hits the stop price, the order converts into a limit order. Stop-limit order guarantees you a price limit. On the other hand, it also guarantees that an order is executed but not at the stop order rate. A stop-limit order also deals with the problems that a stop order doesn't tackle.

A trader owns a stock that is trading at $20. He would sell it if the price takes a dip below $15 but only if the stock can be sold at $14 or more than that. He would set the stop-limit order by fixing the stop price at $15 and the limit price at $14. That's how no matter how fast the market is dropping, your order will be executed not below $14 because you have set a limit on the execution of the order.

Trailing Stop Order

A trailing stop order is akin to a stop order. However, it works based on a percentage change in the market price as opposed to the target price. A trailing stop order is linked to a long position but it can also be used with a shorter position. In this case, the stock is likely to be purchased if its price increases on the back of a determined percentage. An investor buys a stock for $20. He places a trailing stop order by 20%. If the stock tends to drop by 20% or more than that, the order is likely to be executed.

Market-If-Touched Orders

These are quite similar to limit orders except for the fact that they don't guarantee a price. This helps in the quick execution of order while at the same time allowing investors to set the target prices instead of buying at the market price. The trader needs to set a price and if the stock hits that price, the MIT order will convert into a market order.

A trader is looking to buy a stock that is valued at $20 but he doesn't want to pay that much for that. He places an MIT order with the target price of $15. When the stock sinks to $15, the MIT order converts into a market order and the trader will purchase the stock. As an MIT order tends to convert into a market order, it carries along with the risks of market orders after conversion. There is a high risk of slippage which you need to keep in mind as a trader.

Limit-If-Touched (LIT) Orders

A Limit-If-Touched (LIT) order is just like the MIT order. However, it is different in the sense that it sends forward a limit order instead of a market order. LIT orders are generally different from the standard limit orders because the trader has the power to set the trigger price and the limit price as well.

A stock is trading at $10.50. You can place a LIT buy order at $10.40. The limit price can be set at $10.35. If the price drops to $10.40 or lower than that, the limit order will be placed at $10.35. As it is a limit order, you will only be able to buy the shares at $10.35 or less than that. If you cannot find buyers who are willing to sell at that price, the order will fail to execute even though the LIT price has reached (Milton, 2020).

How to Place an Order?

Trading or investment in a stock is done by buying a certain number of shares of a company. The order stays incomplete when you place it until you can see a change in the order status. There are several online trading platforms that you can use to make the purchase. You also can place an order through a direct telephone call to your broker.

Buy Orders

Buy orders are the ones that are placed when the price of a share is likely to rise in the short or long run, which means a hold period of a few minutes to a few hours. This is about the demand-supply curve in the share market. When the demand for a stock rises in the open market, the price is likely to rise significantly. As the price takes off to a higher spot, day traders see a further rise and enter their buying positions.

Sell Orders

Sell orders are executed when an investor feels that the price of the share is likely to decline in the short run. However, it is based on analysis and market predictions. Market depth alludes to the number of Buy and Sell orders at different price levels at a particular point in time. You can analyze the bid quantity with the bid price. In the end, you have a Total Buy Quantity. Similarly, you can analyze the ask price and the ask quantity to view the Total Sell Quantity.

Order Execution

Orders are usually executed by a broker on your behalf. The broker charges an amount to execute the orders. In an electronic platform, the orders are executed automatically.

Contract Notes

A contract note is generally a written agreement between the broker and the investor for the flawless execution of trade transactions. Contract note can be sent through an automated message or via mail. A contract note contains the name of a transaction, charges of the brokers, trading registration number of the broker, the settlement number, and a digital signature done by the broker.

Chapter 9: Strategies to Minimize Risk While Trading

Risk management helps you cut down on your losses in the trading market. It also can help traders protect their accounts from losing all the money. The risk occurs when a trader suffers from a loss. If you can manage it properly, you give yourself another opportunity to make money in the market. It is an essential but more often overlooked prerequisite of day trading. A trader who has succeeded in generating substantial profits may lose it all in a single bad trade if he doesn't have a risk management strategy in place. So, how can you develop the top techniques to curb the market?

Trading usually is considered as exciting and profitable if you manage to keep your focus intact, do necessary diligence, and keep your emotions at bay. Still, top traders ought to incorporate risk management practices for the prevention of losses from shooting out of control. If you build a strategic and objective approach to cut down on your losses with the help of stop orders or wise profit-taking, you can stay in the game for a long time.

Plan Trades

You cannot win a battle without proper planning. Just like everything else in life, you need to properly plan your trade. Planning is the difference between success and failure. The first thing is to make sure that your broker is the right person for your trading ventures. Some brokers charge high commissions but they don't offer the right tools for analysis. Analytical tools are something that day traders must keep in possession. You need those tools to cut down on your risks. Stop-loss or take-profit generally represent the two key ways in which traders can plan when they are trading. You must know at which price you want to buy and at which you want to sell. Better keep a notebook in which you can write the buy and sell price. There should be no gambling or being a lucky thing. When people face losses, they desperately try to bring their money back, which causes them to lose more money. Similarly, profits entice day traders to hold on to their active positions for a longer period to make more money.

The One-Percent Rule

Many day traders follow the one-percent rule. This suggests that you should not put over 1% of your capital in a single trade. If you have $10,000 in your trading account, you should only invest $100 in a single trade. Many traders follow this strategy especially. You also can if you have less than $100,000 in your trading account. Some traders go over 2% if the market seems to be bright. However, that's not recommended. When you break a rule, you have to pay for the damages. The standard is to keep the trading positions below 2%.

Set Stop-loss

A stop-loss, as already defined, is the price at which a trader sells the stock and posts a loss in a trade. This happens when a trade doesn't go the way the trader wanted it to go. Most traders sell a stock if its price breaks below a key support level. You need to set the stop-loss points effectively. You can do that by using your analytical tools as well, but a fundamental analysis of the particular stock can help you set the timing of the stop-loss.

You can use long-term moving averages for the stocks that have a higher level of volatility to lower the chances that a meaningless swing in price will trigger a stop-loss order to be executed. You also need to adjust the moving averages to match the price ranges. If the price range is longer, you need to use longer moving averages to minimize the risks. Stop losses need not be closer than 1.5 times the current high-to-low range (volatility) as they are likely to be executed without any reason. You also need to adjust the stop loss according to the volatility of the trading market. If the price is not shaking much, the stop-loss points can be tightened.

Diversification

You need to make sure that most of your trading means that you are never putting all of your eggs in one basket. If you are investing a major chunk of your capital in one instrument, you are setting the stage for yourself to make a big loss in a short window of time. The most viable risk management strategy that suits day traders is to diversify the portfolio across different industry sectors and geographical regions.

Reward-Risk Ratio

When you detect a particular entry signal, you need to think where you can place a stop loss. Take your profit first. Once you have identified reasonable price levels for your orders, you can measure the reward: risk ratio. The takeaway is that the reward of a trade is uncertain. It is the risk that you can control about your trade.

Avoid Volatile Conditions

The rule of the thumb is that you ought to avoid volatile conditions in the market. It may seem off the track as day traders wait for volatile conditions to enter the market and make big profits. They think that volatility is good for their business as it allows big fluctuations in the price of stocks and offers big profits. Yes, it is a fact that volatility brings some great opportunities. Here, the point is that you need to avoid short-term volatility that is linked to a new event or an unknown occurrence that tends to swing the market for a while. These kinds of events are considered as high-risk events in the world of stocks. They can cause a higher level of pip movement in a matter of seconds. You cannot have an edge during these short windows. Take a break from trading during these jumps, if you have entered a position, you should cut down on the risk by lowering down the size of your position. You will not like to get entangled in a position during these momentary swings in the market that would go as fast as they came.

A Higher Timeframe

One type of risk that lots of day traders despise to discuss is the risk that is associated with overtrading. Traders focus on short-term strategies because they think that the more they trade, the higher is the profit. This is just not true and this can be dangerous for you. You need to be patient and keep a two to three hours trading window to see which direction a certain trade goes. This is how you can minimize your transaction costs. A transaction cost can be defined as a form of bid-ask spreads along with commissions. They can take a heavy toll on the profits you make in the market.

Forex Risk Management

Forex risk management is considered as one of the top debated topics in the realm of trading. On the one hand, traders lookout for a reduction in the size of potential losses while on the other hand, they want to make big profits out of each trading position. There is a common belief that you have to take greater risks to get higher returns.

The reason why lots of traders lose money in Forex is that they have a lack of experience in managing risk. Forex market is highly volatile which makes it inherently risky. Therefore, risk management in Forex ensures success even for beginners. It is estimated that Forex is a $5.1 trillion US dollar market. It encompasses financial establishments, banks, and independent bankers in its loop. The size of the market provides immense profit-making opportunities and risks as well. Here is a rundown of the risks involved in Forex trading.

- The first risk is the market risk which can be defined as the market that performs the other way than you had expected. For example, if expect the US dollar to rise against EUR, the opposite will happen and you post a loss.

- Forex offers hefty leverage to traders which raises profits as well as losses. You can buy a larger number of trades than you have money in the account which increases the chances of your loss.

- Some currencies are inherently liquid. Supply and demand differ for them. Trades are executed in these currencies in a fast manner. Similarly, some currencies are low in liquidity. Trading in highly liquid currencies means that trades are not executed at the expected price as there is usually a delay in the execution because of the higher number of trades.

Limit Leverage

This is the most important aspect of trading in Forex. You can put a limit on using leverage. Leverage in Forex offers you an opportunity to amplify your profits from your trading account. At the same time, it raises the risk factor. There is a leverage of 1:200 which means that if you have $400 in your account, you can trade with $80,000. Similarly, if you have $800, you can trade with $160,000. This means that if the trade moves in your favor, you are likely to earn a big amount of cash, but if it goes against you, you are likely to lose an equally big amount of money. Your level of exposure to risk is greater than the leverage itself. As a beginner, you should avoid high leverages. The market data for leverages differ according to trader status. As a retail trader, you can afford to take the leverage of 1:30. Don't go for more than that if you don't want to wash your hands of your account and profits.

No one can predict which way Forex will move but you do have plenty of evidence from the past trades about how the markets react in certain conditions. What has happened in the past is unlikely to be repeated in the future but it does give you an insight into how you should react to these situations.

Conclusion

Trading is gradually exploding into a profession. There have been lots of courses and seminars regularly being conducted on the importance and the techniques of day trading. All these educational materials and courses are aimed at raising the level of your education in the field of trading. The key to master the art of day trading is maintaining knowledge and discipline. When you are sitting in front of your trading computer screen with your finger on the trigger, you are about to take decisions in split seconds. Your decisions can help you rake in thousands of dollars while at the same time, it can strip you of thousands of dollars.

Day trading does not care about how good looking you are and how you live your life. It depends on how well you deal with your single trades. It doesn't matter how efficient your broker is or highly literate your friends are. Instead, it depends on how in-depth your knowledge is and how well you utilize the same knowledge in executing your trades.

As you have completed your journey through the book, I have an advice for you which is that you should do your research on each stock that attracts you. Read high-quality books and research papers. Attend high-quality seminars. Trading is not something that you can learn overnight. It takes sweat, determination, focus, and lots of reading. Also, you start with a tiny capital to learn the ways of the stock market through the first-hand experience. You should let the market itself teach you. This technique is the cheapest and most effective way of learning.

What you have learned in the book, can be applied and tested in the stock market with a little capital. When you come across a term or a graph throughout your journey in the stock market, you can apply it in the real stock market. Take a closer look at the results. See how well you were able to apply the techniques that you have learned and what were the results of these techniques. Also, see what was the speed of your execution in the market? People don't come in slow when a stock gets volatile or when a piece of news breaks out.

I had a friend who lost $50k in the stock market just because he was overconfident. He scanned some common material on day trading and convinced himself that he was a master now. This led him to trade crazily. He would day trade like a mad man, jumping from one trade to another to bring back the lost money and to make profits. He failed in the end and once he admitted that, he went on to get proper knowledge about day trading.

The key to successful day trade, as he explains now, is to be in the right head. He says that the only method to survive is doing the right calculations. He emphasizes that day traders should include all methods and strategies into a consolidated whole. He stresses the importance of executing each trade after careful deliberation. As far as I can tell he mastered the art of diversification, low leverage, and reading through the volume.

Your journey through the end of the book shows your determination and courage. I trust that you are now on the way to becoming a brilliantly successful trader. I wrote each word of this book with due consideration with the hope that it will change the lives of people. I hope the strategies and methods that I have given in the book will turn out to be highly beneficial for you. Prosperous are the ones who never cease to learn.

I hope the tricks that I have mentioned in the book will save you from losing your capital and will help you double it in a short time. Always trust your analysis and then listen to your gut. Be patient and emotionally stable when you enter a position. Any step taken in desperation will dent your capital. Loss is a part of the stock market. If you are not losing a position, you are not learning anything. Even seasoned traders go through chaos when they lose money by betting on bad stocks. Don't be afraid of that. What matters is that you learn to survive tough times and then capitalize on the fruitful conditions in the market. Have a happy day trading journey!

References

Maybury, M. (2016). Day Trading A Beginners Guide [pdf]. Retrieved from https://www.pdfdrive.com/day-trading-a-beginners-guide-to-day-trading-learn-the-day-trading-basics-to-building-riches-e196734728.html

Mitchell, C. (Oct 21, 2018). Pros and Cons of Day Trading Versus Long-term Investing. Retrieved from https://www.thebalance.com/day-trading-versus-long-term-investing-4139868

Stock Market Day Trading. (n.d). Retrieved from https://www.jobmonkey.com/daytrading/advantages/

Bajpai, P. (Jun 25, 2019). Day-Trading Tips for Rookies. Retrieved from https://www.investopedia.com/articles/active-trading/071414/day-trading-rules-rookies-dont-play-it-ear.asp

Hall, M. (Aug 18, 2019). How to Choose Stocks for Day Trading. Retrieved from https://www.investopedia.com/financial-edge/0612/how-to-choose-stocks-for-day-trading.aspx

Mcdowell, B. (Mar 19, 2009). This is the mindset of a successful trader. Retrieved from https://tradingmarkets.com/recent/this_is_the_mindset_of_a_successful_trader-641229.html

Edwood, F. (Mar 3, 2020). High-Frequency Trading, Explained. Retrieved from https://cointelegraph.com/explained/high-frequency-trading-explained

Sykes, T. (April 10, 2020). Penny Stocks Trading For Beginners. Retrieved from https://www.timothysykes.com/penny-stocks/

Common exit strategies in trading. (Nov 20, 2018). Retrieved from https://capital.com/common-exit-strategies-in-trading

Konchar, P. (October 10, 2019). What is volatility? And strategies to trade it. Retrieved from https://www.mytradingskills.com/volatility-trading-strategies

Milton, A. (April 13, 2020). Trading Order Types. Retrieved from https://www.thebalance.com/trading-order-types-1031050

www.ingramcontent.com/pod-product-compliance
Lightning Source LLC
Chambersburg PA
CBHW052354220526
45465CB00003BA/1102